CATHERINE MACKENZIE

CHRISTIAN
HEROES

JUST LIKE YOU

CF4•K

Copyright © Catherine Mackenzie 2021

paperback ISBN 978-1-5271-0678-9
epub ISBN 978-1-5271-0743-4
mobi ISBN 978-1-5271-0744-1

10 9 8 7 6 5 4 3 2 1

Published in 2021
by
Christian Focus Publications Ltd,
Geanies House, Fearn, Ross-shire,
IV20 1TW, Scotland, Great Britain

www.christianfocus.com

Cover design by Pete Barnsley

Printed and bound by Gutenberg, Malta

CONTENTS

Young readers, as well as more seasoned ones, require a consistent feast of spiritual nurture, and Catherine MacKenzie places a rich entree on the table in *Christian Heroes - Just Like You and Me*. An insightful tour of many key figures in church history, this little book helps others to see just how God worked through those He chose to face critical moments. Catherine expertly weaves together the magnificence and flaws of these individuals, helping young people see that God indeed works through fallen yet hopeful believers, as He can through each of us today.

Rev. Luke H. Davis,
Bible Department Chairman, Westminster Christian Academy, St. Louis, Missouri

We need heroes to inspire us in our daily lives. In Catherine MacKenzies' *Christian Heroes - Just Like You* we are introduced to twenty-one heroes from the 1st century to the present who are an inspiration. Their main focus in life was to serve God, even in difficult circumstances. However, MacKenzie has wisely shown the reader the flaws in these all too human heroes, which is also inspiring. She shows us that God can use his people to do his work and bring glory to his name in spite of their feet of clay.

Linda Finlayson, author, Philadelphia

Reading Catherine Mackenzie's *Christian Heroes—Just Like You* took me back to teenage years and my first encounters with many of the extraordinary men whose life stories she retells. Their commitment to Christ, their struggles to grow to be more like him, as well as many of the books they wrote, have been a lifelong inspiration and challenge. I hope that learning about them in these pages will have a similar effect on many young people today. Just Like Us is a great way for anyone to learn more about what it means to trust, love, follow and serve the Lord.

Sinclair B. Ferguson
Ligonier Ministries teaching fellow and Chancellor's Professor of Systematic Theology at Reformed Theological Seminary

'A book about ordinary, everyday heroes who powerfully shaped Christianity with their quills, pens, stories, voices, and even their blood! If you want a life that revolves around you - DON'T READ THIS BOOK! These historical profiles are hazardous for those who want to waste their lives.'

Natalie Brand
Tutor for Women
Union School of Theology

Just like you and me?

When you think about the men and women of the past you might think of people who wore strange clothes or did things differently to the way we do things today. They didn't even have plumbing in those days, yes? Most could not read or write? Well, that's not exactly true. The Romans managed to transport fresh water into their cities and even though they were poor fishermen the disciples wrote down the truth of the gospel. So, they were possibly not as backward and uncivilised as we might think. The men and women of history weren't that different to us after all. That's one reason why it is good to find out about the lives of Christians who have gone before – they were human like you and me, they did their best and sometimes made mistakes. They also needed to learn from the Word of God as we do. That is something that never changes throughout history. The gospel that Polycarp preached in Smyrna, that Hudson Taylor taught in China and that you need to believe today is the same gospel. Jesus Christ is the same Saviour.

As you read the real-life stories of these amazing people you will realise that they were young men keen for adventure, as well as quiet studious types. Some were physically strong, but some were sick and poorly. Some longed for adventure, others enjoyed a library and a big cup of tea. They were all heroes in their own way, but they also had flaws – just like us. They were ordinary people who were given the gift of faith – faith in the one true God.

Some of these men showed great bravery in the most dreadful circumstances. As we find out where their strength comes from, we will discover that this same strength is waiting for us to use in our lives. God is the same yesterday, today and forever. It is his strength that these Christians relied on. He will be your strength too.

1
Polycarp
(65—156)

Polycarp was bishop of the church in Smyrna in Asia Minor.
Polycarp died as a martyr.

Have you ever wished that you had seen the miracles that Jesus performed? It would have been amazing to have heard about Jesus from the lips of people who actually saw the feeding of the 5,000 or who witnessed Jairus' daughter being raised to life! How about actually meeting with someone who had witnessed the resurrection!

Some people, like the disciples, did all this. The Apostle John had a student named Polycarp who went on to be a leader in the Early Church. Because of his friendship with John, Polycarp had access to someone who had actually seen and heard Jesus Christ in person. Polycarp had many opportunities to ask John about what had happened then.

When Polycarp heard the good news of Jesus he was convinced of the truth of this message – that Jesus Christ was the Son of God, had died on the cross and had risen to life. He knew that it was through the sacrifice of Christ's death and the power of his resurrection that he, Polycarp could be saved from sin to eternal life.

Polycarp had not physically seen Jesus for himself, but through God's Word he met him spiritually and became his follower. Polycarp then had to pass the same message onto others. Today, if you are able to read the truth of God's Word, you are part of a chain of people that extends from the time of the resurrection through the days of the Early Church, medieval times, the Reformation and on to the day when Jesus finally returns, as he has promised in God's Word.

You are part of a story that involves disciples, saints and martyrs – and one of those martyrs was Polycarp.

By the time Polycarp was an elderly man he had become bishop of the church in Smyrna, an area that is now part of what we call Turkey. Polycarp had been born into a world dominated by the Roman Empire: a superpower whose tentacles eventually spread out across Europe, North Africa and the Middle East. The empire was ruled from a city in Central Italy called Rome and was ruled by a single emperor. The world that Polycarp lived in was not an easy one, especially if you were a Christian. Christians believed in the one true God. The Roman culture believed in a multitude of gods and they even worshipped their own emperors as gods. If you were a Christian and refused to make sacrifices to the emperor or worship him, you would have definitely faced persecution.

The city of Smyrna was at the centre of one of those persecutions. Christians began to lose their lives because of their faith. Some were willing to turn away from their faith to save their lives. But Polycarp was not.

For his own safety, his congregation urged Polycarp to leave the city before the persecution got too much.

Reluctantly, Polycarp left to find shelter in a farmhouse where he would hopefully be safe. The punishment for being a Christian was now death in public – a spectacle that was organised by the Roman authorities for the amusement of its citizens. Amphitheatres like the Colosseum in Rome were built wherever Rome flexed its power. And it was within these centres of amusement that many Christians suffered and died. They were treated like common criminals and killed in very cruel ways. If it wasn't by crucifixion, it was by animals like boars, wild dogs or lions.

Sadly, Polycarp's secret hideout didn't remain secret for long. One Friday as the local Smyrna citizens were enjoying their usual gruesome amusements, someone thought it would be fun to demand the death of Polycarp – the local Christian bishop. The chant went up and so the search was started to find the elderly man in order to please the crowds. It was only after they tortured two of Polycarp's servants that they discovered where he was hiding.

Polycarp wasn't surprised when they arrived. He'd had a dream that he would die a martyr's death – not by the sword, a cross, or by wild beasts – but by flames. In his dream he had felt his pillow on fire and knew that that was how he would die. When his captors arrived at the farm to arrest him, Polycarp didn't panic. He gently invited his captors in for some food and drink, politely requesting one hour alone with God to pray. They give him his wish before marching him to the arena. He was given one last chance to change his mind and renounce Christ, to which Polycarp replied, 'Eighty-six years I have served him. He has never done me wrong. How then can I blaspheme my King who has saved me?' The threat of being burned alive would not persuade Polycarp to desert his Saviour, 'You threaten fire that burns for an hour and is over. But the judgment on the ungodly is forever.'

Polycarp was then tied up and set alight.

His last prayer was, 'O Lord God Almighty, Father of thy beloved and blessed Child, Jesus Christ, ... I bless Thee, that Thou hast granted me this day and hour ... I praise Thee for all things, I bless Thee, I glorify Thee through the everlasting and heavenly High Priest, Jesus Christ, thy beloved Child, through whom be glory to Thee with Him and the Holy Spirit, both now and for the ages that are to come, Amen.'

Things to do:
1. On a map look up the area of Turkey and Smyrna.
2. In a dictionary find the definition of the word 'persecution' – find out about the persecuted church today.
3. Look up the following Scripture: John 15:8. How does this verse help and encourage those who are persecuted for their faith in Christ?

2

Athanasius

(c. 293–373)

Athanasius was the 20th Bishop of Alexandria, a Christian theologian, Church Father, and an Egyptian.

When you hear a politician or business tycoon speak, they can sound impressive and very believable. Then you hear someone who disagrees with them and you change your opinion. We have been given minds and intelligence to weigh up different points of view and God allows us to decide about day-to-day questions such as who should govern, and what they should do about taxes, or the law.

But there are other more important questions that are clearly answered in God's Word and that should not be doubted, disobeyed or changed in anyway. Such as the fact that Jesus Christ is 'the way, the truth, and the life: no man cometh unto the Father, but by him' (John 14:6). When you hear someone speak against the Word of God you can be certain they are wrong and not to be trusted. We must read God's Word in order to understand what is true and what are lies.

Athanasius was born at a time in history when key doctrines of the Christian faith such as the identity of Jesus Christ and God himself were being challenged within the church, but from the very beginning of Athanasius' life God was preparing him to be a defender of the faith.

Athanasius was born to a Christian family around the year 293. Over time, Christianity had gained more acceptance in the Roman world, but the church and its leaders still found themselves in conflict with emperors from without and heretics from within.

Athanasius came from a Christian family that was rich enough to give him a fine education, but they were not of the highest class in his society. This might seem like a disadvantage, but in reality it meant that Athanasius spoke and wrote in the language of the people, rather than the highly educated way that high class Romans did.

He was fluent in the Egyptian language of Coptic, as well as Greek and, though it's not clear where he was born, he was living in the city of Alexandria from quite a young age. An interesting story is told about him as a boy. A church leader was one day watching children playing at 'church'. Athanasius was one of them. He had been pretending to baptise his companions. The church leader, Alexander, told him to stop, as it was important not to do these things without first teaching the truth of God's Word. However, something about Athanasius must have captured that church leader's attention, as he asked him and some of the other lads to think about making the church their career.

And this is what Athanasius did. He eventually became the bishop's personal secretary at the first Council of Nicea: a very important meeting of church officials. It was at this meeting that the church agreed a creed which declared the divine nature of God the Son and his relationship to God the Father.[1] Athanasius then replaced Bishop Alexander when he retired, even though there was a lot of opposition from the followers of a particular heretic called Arius.

Arius was one of those challengers to the truth of God's Word who caused great division in the early Christian church. Arius did not believe that Jesus Christ was God. People who thought the same, soon came to be called Arians. They believed that when Jesus was born he had only been the first and greatest of created beings, that he was not actually divine. This was wrong and is what we call heresy.

Athanasius argued effectively against the Arian heresy. He particularly focussed on 2 Peter 1:4 where Peter describes Christians as 'partakers of the divine nature'. By the grace of God, humanity could now share in God's glory and in eternal life. Athanasius argued that because this was true, then Jesus Christ had to be God. How could Jesus Christ save sinful humanity and bring them to God's glory, if he was not in actual fact God? Jesus had to be both God and man in one person. Christians were also told to worship Christ. Athanasius astutely pointed out that Christians could not worship Christ unless he was God. Worshipping a created being was idolatry.

Despite Athanasius' intelligence and his ability to defend the truth, the shifts and turns of politics at that time meant that Arius and his supporters persuaded the emperor to banish Athanasius. This happened to Athanasius on five different occasions during his lifetime so that he spent seventeen of his forty-five years as Bishop of Alexandria in exile.

---

1. Nicene Creed.

However, even though Athanasius had been mistreated he was tolerant of those he disagreed with. When there were people who did not believe exactly what he believed he was willing to discuss the issue in the hope that they would eventually come to his opinion or reach a suitable compromise.

In the year 366, Athanasius was finally allowed to return to Alexandria where he spent his last years free of persecution.

Things to do:
1. Find a map and look up the country of Egypt. Can you find the city of Alexandria which still exists today?
2. In the dictionary find the definition of the words 'creator' and 'created'.
3. Look up Genesis 1:26 – this verse demonstrates the truth that God is one God but three persons. How is that? Look up these verses too: Matthew 3:16; Matthew 28:19; Colossians 2:9; Ephesians 2:18; Isaiah 48:16.

3

Augustine

(354—430)

Augustine was born in Algeria. He was a theologian, philosopher and bishop.

Augustine was born in the town of Thagaste and had a loving mother, whose name was Monica. Though his father was a pagan, and worshipped many different gods, Augustine's mother was a believer in the Lord Jesus Christ. The one thing that she longed for, more than anything else, was for her own son to know the same Saviour as she did. She prayed earnestly that he would turn to trust in the one true God. She wept bitterly over her young son. Augustine's conversion was not what you might call straightforward.

Some of the people who looked after Augustine as a chubby little baby, loved God and taught him about God's love and care. And though he is now remembered as an important leader of the Early Church, when he was little he was just a typical baby fussing and crying for attention. In Augustine's autobiography he describes that when he was a baby, all he could do was suck, or sleep, or cry when he didn't get what he wanted. However, it wasn't his family's fault that he cried. They couldn't always guess what it was he wanted. He would be indignant with his relatives for not giving in to his demands and then take revenge on them by crying even more.

Why do you think Augustine started his autobiography with an anecdote like this? Perhaps he wanted to warn his readership about what was to come. Augustine went through the 'terrible twos' and then he went into the 'terrible teens' and the 'terrible twenties'. Monica was still earnestly praying that the Lord Jesus Christ would bring Augustine to repentance when he was in his thirties.

He received an excellent education, though he wasn't always the most willing student. And despite all the advantages he received as a young man, Augustine was thoughtless and arrogant too. One day Augustine and his friends saw a pear tree in a neighbour's garden. It wasn't a particularly spectacular pear tree and each boy had an even better tree growing in their own gardens, but something inside these lads made them shake the pears off the tree and then start throwing them at some pigs. They had no desire to eat the fruit at all – just cause trouble. Looking back on that incident, Augustine would realise that sin had been the ruler of his life from his earliest years. He saw that he was too easily influenced by the other boys in his circle. The truth was, these friends of his were not really friends at all. 'O friendship too empty of friendship!' Augustine remembered.

The pear tree incident in the end didn't have too serious a consequence for anyone, but it was the beginning of a slippery slope. Augustine grew up and that was when his selfish decisions impacted others.

Augustine decided to live with a young woman who was not his wife. She gave birth to Augustine's son – Adeodatus. Monica was not happy. In those days, marriages were arranged between families. Augustine was living with a girl as if she was his wife and she was not, and he hadn't even asked his family's permission. Sometime later the relationship ended. The young woman was sent away and was separated from Augustine and from her own child. This is a decision we find difficult to understand in our culture today, but Augustine's selfish desires had led to the difficult situation.

In the year 373, Augustine moved to Carthage to be a Professor of Rhetoric which is the art of effective and persuasive speaking or writing. His life was devoted to books and learning, but he could never find the answers that he was looking for. He had big questions about life. Instead of looking in God's Word, though, as he should have done, he joined a sect called the Manichees who rejected the Old Testament. During the nine years that Augustine spent with this group, Monica desperately prayed for his conversion. She asked a friend to try and persuade Augustine that this sect was a lie. The friend could not see Augustine ever being persuaded by argument to believe the truth. Monica would have to continue praying, as it was only God who would bring Augustine to himself. However, as this friend saw Monica in floods of tears, he felt genuinely sorry for her. 'It cannot be that the son of such tears will perish,' he said, trying to comfort her.

Eventually, Augustine did begin to realise that Manichaeism was a false faith. He read other philosophers and beliefs and, although not a Christian, he did come to believe in the existence of one supreme holy God. Augustine became convinced that human beings could know God for themselves.

He heard a preacher named Ambrose and for the first time actually understood the Old Testament. Augustine finally became convinced that Christianity was true. However, Monica's friend had been right – arguments alone would not bring Augustine to faith. He could still not bring himself to give himself to Christ. He did not want to give up the pleasures he enjoyed in order to submit to God.

Then, in the city of Milan, in the year 386, Augustine was relaxing in a garden. He heard a child's voice calling out, 'Take and read! Take and read!' Beside him was a copy of the New Testament so he picked it up and it happened to fall open at the book of Romans where he read Romans 13:13-14 ESV: '... not in orgies and drunkenness, not in sexual immorality and sensuality, not in quarreling and jealousy. But put on the Lord Jesus Christ, and make no provision for the flesh, to gratify its desires.'

Augustine did not need to read any further. 'Instantly, as I finished the sentence, the light of faith flooded into my heart, and all the darkness of doubt vanished.'

It had been a long journey from North Africa to Milan, but a far greater one from doubt to faith. However, the journey wasn't over. Augustine and his son, Adeodatus, were both converted about the same time and baptised together on Easter Sunday 387. Then Augustine went on to become the Bishop of Hippo in North Africa – a preacher, theologian, and a man of great learning. Today, the church owes him a lot through his teachings and writings. Many of the great Reformers and theologians who followed after him were influenced by his teaching of God's truth. He died in the year 430 while the city of Hippo was under siege from an invading Vandal army.

Things to do:

1. Find a map and look up the country of Algeria.

2. In a dictionary find the definition of the word 'conversion' – how does this word describe what happens to a sinner when they come to Christ?

3. Look up the following Scripture: Romans 13:13-14? In what way had Augustine's life before his conversion been simply a pursuit of pleasure and personal glory?

4

Patrick of Ireland

(390—461)

Patrick was a Roman-British Christian bishop and missionary to Ireland.

The Roman world reached far and wide. Its power and influence seemed unstoppable, but by the fourth century Rome's grip of its territories was beginning to weaken. German tribes ransacked key forts on Rome's borders. In the year 410 B.C. the Roman forces stationed in Britain were called to reinforce troops elsewhere in Europe – and they never returned.

What happens when a dictator falls or an occupying power leaves? There is often conflict and chaos. A position of power has been left vacant and there is a struggle, amongst those that remain or by other powers, to replace the power that had been there before.

In the fourth century there were invasions on all sides of the British isles and if you lived on the west coast of Britain at that time, one invader would have been Irish pirates. As a young man, Patrick experienced these pirates in a particularly terrifying way.

We know him today as Patrick of Ireland, but he wasn't born there. It is difficult to know exactly where he was born. Wherever the Roman army went in the British Isles it left a road system allowing them to easily march from one fort to the next. However, after they left, things began to disintegrate even to the extent that some of the places they built are now totally forgotten. Patrick, in his own memories, mentions the name of the place of his birth, yet no one knows for sure where that place was. The best we can say is that it was probably somewhere near Carlisle in Northern England. It was certainly not far from the sea.

Patrick was brought up in a Christian home. Christianity had gained even more acceptance by this time. In the year 311 the emperor of Rome changed the law to protect Christian believers and allow them to worship freely. However, Patrick wasn't yet a believer himself. He knew the Bible stories and could answer questions when asked, but he didn't trust in Jesus for his own salvation. He didn't think he needed to.

Then one day the Irish pirates invaded Patrick's home and Patrick himself was 'taken into captivity in Ireland, along with thousands of others.' This is where we have to use our imaginations a little. It must have been a truly terrifying experience for the young lad, as he was physically dragged away from the safety and security of his home to be sold into slavery in a land across the sea.

Patrick's family prayed for him with tears but had little hope of ever seeing him again. Patrick was truly on his own – although he wasn't, not really, as God was with him. It was at this point that the faith he had been taught as a child really began to mean something to young Patrick personally.

God showed Patrick where his life needed to change. 'I recognised my failings. So I turned with all my heart to the Lord my God and he looked down on my lowliness and had mercy on my youthful ignorance. ... He protected me and consoled me as a father does for his son.'

Patrick's duties as a slave included tending sheep every day. He had to look after these animals, guiding them to pastures and making sure they were protected from wild animals. It would have been hard, cold work, particularly during the winter months, but Patrick used that time to pray. More and more, his love of God increased. 'Faith grew, and my spirit was moved, so that in one day I would pray up to one hundred times, and at night perhaps the same. I even remained in the woods and on the mountain, and I would rise to pray before dawn in snow and ice and rain. I never felt the worse for it, and I never felt lazy – as I realise now, the spirit was burning in me at that time.'

Patrick was a slave in Ireland for several years. Then in his early twenties Patrick had a strange dream. He heard a voice saying to him, 'Very soon you will return to your native country. Look – your ship is ready.' In the dream Patrick saw a ship which was two hundred miles away. He'd never been there before, but he knew how to get there so immediately decided to run away.

It was a long, hard journey over sea and land, but the Lord provided food, fire and shelter every day until Patrick made it back to the loving arms of his parents. They were overjoyed to have their son restored to them, and pleaded that he would never leave them ever again. However, God had other plans. What do you think they were? Where is the last place on earth you would suppose Patrick would go to?

At some point, after escaping from Ireland and being united with his parents, Patrick was given another dream from God. A man whose name was Victoricus approached him with so many letters they could not be counted. They were all from the Irish people and while he was reading them he thought he heard the voices of a great many people calling out with one voice: 'We beg you, holy boy, to come and walk again among us.'

Patrick was greatly moved.

It appeared that God was sending him back to the land of his captivity to proclaim the gospel to lost souls. By this time Patrick had studied in a French monastery and had been given a role of leadership within the church. Patrick packed his bags and returned to preach the gospel to the very people who had kidnapped him as a teenager.

This time he had his freedom, but he was still in danger of his life. Because of his principles and beliefs he refused to accept gifts from the Irish rulers, so Patrick could not call on any of these powerful men to help him when he had need. That meant, though, that when he was attacked and robbed of all he had, Patrick found himself in great danger. He was even put in chains again for a brief time, but thankfully sixty days later he was released.

In the end, Patrick's work in Ireland was a success. He baptised hundreds of people. 'The Irish who had never had the knowledge of God and worshipped only idols and unclean things have now become the Lord's people and are called sons of God.'

Things to do:

1. Find a map and look up the country of Ireland. Find the area of County Down. This is where it is claimed that Patrick built his first church.

2. In a dictionary find the definition of the words 'slave' and 'free'. How in your opinion does the word slave describe someone who does not believe in Christ? How does faith in Christ give us freedom?

3. There are many legends, or unsubstantiated stories about Patrick that may or may not be true. However, it is worth repeating the legend that he attempted to teach the Irish about the doctrine of the Trinity by using a three-leafed clover. Look up the following Bible verses about the Trinity: Luke 1:35; Hebrews 9:14; Peter 1:2.

5

Columba

(521—597)

Columba was an Irish abbot and missionary evangelist credited with spreading Christianity through Scotland. He founded the abbey on Iona.

Sometimes we don't know what people looked like from the past, but as it happens we do know some details about Columba.

Like most monks of that time he would have been simply dressed and his hair was cut in a tonsure. Usually when we hear of that style of hair cut we picture the Roman style of tonsure, where a circle of hair was shaved from off the top of the monk's head. Columba's haircut was similar but different because he was from a branch of the church that was based in Ireland. His tonsure was more towards the front of the head rather than the centre.

He is also described as being lean, sinewy and rather weather-beaten.

Columba was born to a family with aristocratic connections around the year 521 in Donegal, Ireland. Being born with high connections, however, was not as unique or spectacular as you might think. Many young men at that time had claims to the throne of Ireland. So, it's not clear if Columba's connections were of the common sort or if he genuinely was in a position of power through his family.

One of the usual practices in Columba's culture was to send young men off to study at quite a young age. They would be placed in the care of a well-connected individual who would be paid to educate the boy. The young men were taken into these families and treated like a foster child. Originally, they would have joined the family of a pagan priest called a Druid or a poet. Christian families eventually changed that tradition so that they sent their sons into the care of Christian priests – and this is what happened to Columba. After having spent some time being educated in this way it was clear that he had a desire to work in the church, so he took what are called monastic vows. These were promises that he would give his life to the church. He would be obedient and remain unmarried and pure from sexual relations. He would give all his energies to God's kingdom, not amassing riches for his own pleasure. Men who made commitments such as these were called monks and lived in communities, made up of other monks and priests, called monasteries.

The commitments that Columba made were kept for the rest of his life. He was so enthusiastically dedicated to this way of life that he went on to found twenty-five monasteries and forty churches by the time he reached twenty-five years of age.

Now, church heroes like Columba were never perfect. Sometimes their followers in later years wrote about them as if they were, but the truth was often very different. Columba may have had a quick temper. And it is entirely possible that at some point in his story he did something that sparked a feud that caused the deaths of many men. There are hints in history that something like this happened but not a lot of detail. However, it may be that the consequences of Columba's actions meant that he felt ashamed and guilty. Christians at this time in history, if they felt particularly bad about something they had done, would perform 'penance'. This was when Christians did something difficult and costly in order to repent of their sins.

So, it is likely that this is why Columba left Ireland, in his early forties, to share God's truth amongst the pagans in the land we now call Scotland. He left with twelve other monks, firstly to the island of Iona. On the Scottish mainland, Columba's work resulted in the conversion to Christianity of two tribes the Picts and the Scots.

Columba's aristocratic connections in Ireland helped him in his mission to the pagan tribes of Scotland. To gain access to these lands and peoples he had to approach their rulers. The fact that he was at ease in speaking to people of power, meant that he was not intimidated by men like King Bridei. Even though at first some of these rulers did not come to Christ for themselves, they allowed Columba and the other Christians to share the gospel in their lands.

Columba's work shows us that Christian mission is not about what you do or where you do it – it's about the Word of God and the individual people who proclaim that Word. Columba was committed and faithful to the one true God. His life and actions and his preaching were effective in declaring the gospel to the pagan tribes.

When we share God's Word, we don't do so on our own. Columba left Ireland with twelve other men and he joined a Christian work in Scotland that had already begun. So although we are writing about him as a Christian hero, he was part of a team of heroes. When you trust in Christ and follow him you are part of a group of people across the globe who worship together. This is the church.

If you are sharing the gospel today with family and friends you are part of a group of believers, part of a work that goes back to Columba and beyond. It goes back to the day when Jesus himself took his disciples to one side and told them to go into all the world to preach the gospel.

Things to do:
1. Look at the countries of Ireland and Scotland on the map. Find the island of Iona. It is an important place today, but do you think it was important in Columba's time? Why do you think they chose that area to set up their work?
2. In a dictionary look up the word 'penance' and 'repent' – how are these words similar but different?
3. John 2:13-17 – look up this Bible passage. We read about Columba's possible bad temper, but how does Columba's behaviour differ from Jesus Christ? How is the Lord Jesus different to us, but the same? Read Hebrews 4:15.

REFORMERS

6
Martin Luther
(1483—1546)

Martin Luther was a German priest, Augustinian monk and founder of the Reformation

Martin Luther was born to Hans and Margarethe Luther on 10th November, 1483 in Eisleben, a town in Saxony, Germany. Coming from strong Saxon stock, the Luthers were more peasant than middle class, but Martin's father had ambitious plans. The Luthers moved to a town called Mansfield in 1484 and soon Hans was the proud owner of six copper mines and had been elected as a town councillor. His schemes didn't end there. In the 1400s your family fortunes increased through your children, in particular your sons. Daughters were married off to other families with the hope that they would no longer be a burden, but sons remained to run the family farm or business. If your family was fortunate, one son or two would leave to study the law or join the church. The church could be a lucrative choice of career for a gifted young man, but Hans wanted his son Martin to study law. He did not want him to become a monk. His plans involved a wife and family for Martin, not monastic vows.

Martin went to various schools and ended up in Magdeburg in 1497, then Eisenach in 1498. The young boy didn't exactly enjoy his studies for a variety of reasons. One was that most days he was ravenously hungry. Students in the Middle Ages were sent away from their families and often neglected by the people who were supposed to care for them. One of the practices of young boy students at that time was to wander through the university towns singing for their supper. It was almost like begging. If all went well, they would get some soup or bread to stave off their hunger pangs. If the doors remained closed to them, the young lads went to bed hungry.

When he was seventeen, Martin attended the University of Erfurt where he received his Master's Degree in 1505. This was when it became clear that Martin and his father were not on the same page. After enrolling to study law, Martin dropped out pretty quickly and changed to theology studies. He was looking for something to satisfy an unsettling longing in his soul – but he could not find it. As it turned out, this longing could never be satisfied by mere education.

During this time of anxiety, Martin paid a visit to his parents before making the return journey to university. It was a hot summer's day and before he arrived back at his university accommodation there was a huge thunderstorm. A lightning bolt struck close by, which terrified Martin so much that he called out, 'Help! Saint Anna, I will become a monk!' Luther could not ignore this promise. To the great displeasure of his father, Martin left university, sold his books, and entered an Augustinian Monastery in Erfurt on 17th July, 1505.

Amongst Hans' last words to Martin before he entered the monastery were, 'Have you not heard that you are to honour your father and mother!' However, nothing could persuade Martin to change his mind. His desire for his soul to be at peace was greater than anything. Just as this peace could not be found in education, it would not be found by wearing a monk's habit either.

Martin hoped that by dedicating himself to a life of extreme discipline such as fasting, prayer and confession he would find the release he was desperately searching for. But the monastic life did not bring Martin closer to God. There was thankfully a wise and godly individual in the monastery, Johann von Staupitz, who urged Martin to reconsider his path. He saw how much time Martin spent confessing his sins, depriving himself of food and sleep as he tried to find forgiveness. Johann began to teach Martin that to be truly repentant meant you had to turn away from your sin towards God. It was not about the restrictions and punishment that Martin put on himself. Forgiveness of sins came from a merciful God and a change in Martin's heart.

Sometimes Martin would spend as much as six hours at a time confessing his sins. This infuriated Johann who would sigh and say, 'God is not angry with you. I think you are angry with God! Do you not know that God commands you to hope?'

In 1511, Martin was given the opportunity to visit Rome – the centre of power for the Christian Church at that time. It was during this visit that Martin saw the corruption of the church for himself. Martin muttered an old Italian proverb, 'If there is a hell then Rome is built over it.' He was beginning to see the truth that others, including his father, had already suspected.

Johann von Staupitz introduced Luther to the theology of Augustine and this had a profound effect on him. He came to realise that God chooses undeserving sinners to be saved because of his mercy, not because of their acts.

Then, Martin Luther read Romans 1:17 – 'The righteousness of God.' Before, Martin had always thought that God's righteousness only punished sinners, but then he realised that God's righteousness is something God gives to sinners as a free gift. Christ's righteousness saved you from sin. It was not about what you could do but about what Jesus had already done on the cross.

At the same time, Luther was employed as a theological professor at Wittenberg. While there, Luther discovered that the Pope had given permission to Johann Tetzel, a Dominican friar, to sell indulgences in that area of Germany. Indulgences were pieces of paper that said the purchaser had free entry to heaven. On 31st October, 1517, Luther wrote in protest to his bishop. This letter became known as the Ninety-five Theses. Luther wrote ninety-five arguments, one of which was: 'Why does the pope ... build the basilica of St. Peter with the money of poor believers rather than with his own money?'

Luther pointed out that as forgiveness of sins could only be given by God, then the claim that people could buy freedom from sin's punishment was a lie.

Whether or not this letter was nailed to the castle door in Wittenberg isn't certain, but it is a story that is widely repeated today and has gone down in history as fact. Whatever happened the Theses itself was soon being spread far and wide throughout Germany and across Europe.

It was the beginning of the Reformation. There were great times ahead, a great movement in the people, in the church, in the world. It was the beginning of a great change that saw Martin Luther translate the Bible from Latin into German and begin a movement that opened up the Word of God to be read by the people of God.

In 1520, Martin Luther was excommunicated from the Roman Catholic church and in 1525, to the delight of Luther's father, Luther married an ex Roman Catholic nun named Katherine von Bora. She escaped from her convent in the back of a fishmonger's cart – but that is another story. One of the great things that he and his wife, Katherine, are remembered for in the Reformed Church today is their example of a loving Christian marriage and family life.

As with anyone, Martin Luther has his achievements and his failures, his joys and his sorrows. He is noted for saying controversial things, sometimes insensitive even. He definitely suffered from depression to the extent that his wife would sometimes rebuke him for it. The fact that Luther is a theological giant is indisputable, but he was also a Christian with some views that we find difficult to swallow today.

He is an example of someone in history that we must be thankful for, but at the same time we are to read the words he wrote and the quotes and sayings that are reported about him with great care. I'm certain that Martin would have agreed with that. We need to read the lives and works of history's Christians in the light of God's Word. Where their lives proclaim God's glory we rejoice and where they don't, we must ask God to give us faith and wisdom to learn from their mistakes.

Things to do:
1. Find a map of Germany today and work out what countries are on its borders.
2. Look up the word 'reformation' in the dictionary and write down the definition. Does the church need a reformation today do you think?
3. Look up the verse that Martin Luther read: Romans 1:16-17.

SOMETHING EXTRA

Reformation means change – so why did the church in the 1400s need to change as much as it did?

Here are two things that had gone wrong:

1. The church had added to the Word of God. They had adopted rituals and traditions that were not part of God's law. It probably happened slowly at first, and may have almost been unnoticeable. However, over time some of the extra things that the church had decided were good ideas became more important than the actual truth of God. The importance given to monasteries and convents and the vows taken by monks were elevated to an importance that they shouldn't have been. It became worse than that – false teaching also crept in. The church became rich and powerful and in order to keep its properties and riches, and to build bigger and better palaces and cathedrals, more money was needed.

One of the most horrendous lies that the church leadership promoted was the lie of purgatory and indulgences. The church falsely proclaimed that individuals could purchase a place in heaven by paying for something called an indulgence. Those who didn't, would suffer for a long time in a place called purgatory when they died. This is a lie. Salvation is not gained through money or actions. We are saved only through Christ's death and sacrifice. It is a free gift from God. However, the church leadership at that time peddled this lie in order to fill its coffers. The cathedral of St. Peter's in Rome was largely built through the money gained by such deceit. And that leads to the other thing that had tragically gone wrong in the church.

2. It had lost its moral compass, as we would say today. Men who were in positions of authority in the church lived godless lives. If you do a historical tour of Rome you will be shown impressive buildings that were the last word in luxury in their day. These palaces were built for the illegitimate children of cardinals and popes. The church leadership gave too much importance to the vows of chastity and poverty taken by its monks and nuns – but hypocritically did not obey the vows themselves.

There were many people who were disgusted at the double standards they saw coming out of Rome but faced with such power and authority what could they do? Men like Martin Luther wanted the church to reform, to change so that it once again gave glory to God.

Their words and actions started a movement we now call the Reformation. The Reformation continues today with people who protect the church and the truth of God's Word. Men like Martin Luther began it, men like John Calvin and John Owen defended it. People like you and I should proclaim it by continually reading God's Word and living by it.

7

John Calvin

(1509–1564)

John Calvin was a French theologian, pastor and Reformer in Geneva during the Protestant Reformation.

John Calvin was a different personality to other people, even other Reformers and he had different gifts. Calvin's life shows that in the story of the church God uses people from all backgrounds. He gives gifts and talents to some and not others, to them he gives different abilities and strengths.

What was Calvin's gift? It was clearly his mind and his pen.

The Reformation began in Germany, but it spread to other countries such as England, Scotland and France. And it was in France that John Calvin was born and educated. His education meant that instead of being crushed to a footnote in history, the Reformation became a turning point of nations.

John Calvin was born in Noyon, a town in Picardy, France, on the 10th of July, 1509. He had an older brother and a younger one and tragically their mother died when John was still quite young. Calvin's father, Gérard, worked as a lawyer or notary and had ambitions for his three sons to make their livings by joining the church. Calvin's father paid money, and made connections in order to advance the careers of his sons. John was particularly intelligent so Gérard made sure that John counted among his friends and study partners the sons of rich gentlemen.

We would consider the age of fourteen a bit young to be sent away to university, but in the 1500s it was quite common to start a university education at that age. Calvin went to Paris and by the year 1523 we find him studying at College Montaigu. And by 1527, Calvin's eyes were opened to the thoughts behind the Reformation. Luther was in his reading pile and others who had discovered Reformed thinking had become his close friends.

Calvin's father, however, changed his mind about sending his son into the church. He decided that it would be better for John to become a lawyer. By the time this story reaches the next decade, Calvin is a qualified lawyer and has firmly nailed his colours to the mast of the Reformation. Calvin realised he was a lost sinner in need of salvation – a salvation that came from Christ alone.

By 1532, Calvin found himself on the run for his beliefs. He had supported a friend who had publicly spoken up for the need to reform the church. Calvin then had to flee France and retreat to Basel. Four years later, Calvin published the first edition of his book *The Institutes of the Christian Religion* – a defence of his faith and a statement of the doctrine of the Reformation. It wasn't intended to be a heavy theological book but something that could be read by anyone interested in Christianity. This book became his major work as he set about editing it and adding to it for rest of his life.

Sometime later, he made plans to move to Strasbourg but due to circumstances beyond his control he was forced to change route and head for Geneva. He intended to stay there for only one night, but Calvin's plans were drastically changed by another French Reformer who stayed there – William Farrell. Persuasive and definitely a bit of a hot head, Farrell pleaded with Calvin to stay and help the Reformed cause in Geneva. Unfortunately, although the city of Geneva was a Protestant city, Calvin's views for reform were more radical than many could stomach – at least at that time. The Geneva Council finally kicked both Calvin and Farrell out. By September 1538 Calvin had accepted a pastorate in Strasbourg.

His congregation was about 500 individuals and he preached every day and twice on the Lord's Day. Calvin also spent a considerable amount of time writing, but his congregation thought it would be better if he spent more time looking for a wife. At first reluctant Calvin came up with lots of excuses for turning down the women who were suggested to him as suitable marriage partners. However, in 1540, he married a widow, Idelette de Bure, who also had two children from her first marriage. She and Calvin had other children of their own but none of them survived infancy.

On 13th September, 1541, after considerable negotiations and pleadings, Calvin was persuaded to return to the city of Geneva. The people there realised that they needed the pastor they had decided to kick out. However, Calvin's vision was not just for the church but for the city itself to be reformed. This involved him bringing reform to not just the church but to the political and social sphere too. Calvin persuaded the city council to enforce legislation against adultery, prostitution, drunkenness, gambling, swearing, and disobedience to parents amongst other things.

The amazing thing is that Calvin achieved all these changes simply through the spoken word. He never held an official position of power and was never a member of the city council

– yet he had the ability to persuade others that reform and radical reform was what was needed.

There was one man, however, whom he could never persuade although he earnestly tried, a man named Michael Servetus, a brilliant Spanish scholar. This man declared the Trinity to be 'a three-headed monster'. And this was a heresy abhorred by both Protestant and Catholic alike.

Calvin did not sign the death sentence as some make out that he did. He wasn't a recognised citizen of Geneva at this point, so had no power or authority. He had more mercy than the city council, as he would have preferred Servetus to have undergone a swift death rather than the one he eventually suffered. This incident in Calvin's life is difficult for us to understand in modern times. However, the solemn fact is that the sentence of death would have been carried out in any city across Europe during this period. Servetus was flouting a core creed of the church: the Nicean Creed. Before he was burned at the stake Calvin visited Servetus several times in order to persuade him to renounce his heresy, but he wouldn't.

This incident is one that haunts the legacy of Calvin even today. If our Christian heroes and heroines displayed some sort of fantastical perfection it would be hard to believe they existed. However, these men and women from the past were not fairy tales, or fiction but real. They had real failings and real problems as we do. It is just easier to spot those issues in the life of someone else rather than ourselves.

Calvin didn't wield a sword like others did – his weapon was his word and that was the legacy he left. Through it he gave the Protestant church a crucial book in *The Institutes* which clearly laid out what Reformed theology was. He reformed the way that the church was governed while also reforming the city of Geneva itself. Under his influence the Reformed faith became an international faith. His influence meant that a great many pastors and missionaries were trained in Geneva and the influence of the Reformation spread still further – even back to John Calvin's native land of France.

Calvin never enjoyed good health and was physically very weak with arthritis and bowel problems. In the year 1558 he caught a fever, and in great pain forced himself to complete the final edition of his Institutes. What had originally started as six chapters, had grown to twenty-one and then eighty. He also continued to preach, which brought on a final decline in his condition. John Calvin died on the 27th of May, 1564, at fifty-four years of age. He was deliberately buried in an unmarked grave in the Cimetière des Rois. A stone, however, has since been placed on a spot that is traditionally thought to be Calvin's grave-site. Even in the last memorial that the world would have of the great Reformer, Calvin did not want people to mistakenly give undue attention to his remains. Today his theology is described as Calvinism – something that I am afraid the Reformer himself would not have been that keen on.

Things to do:

1. Find an atlas and with your finger draw a line from where John Calvin was born in Noyon, to where he studied in Paris, then to Basel, Geneva and Strasbourg then back to Geneva.

2. In a dictionary look up the definition of the word 'legacy'. What do you think most people think of as legacy, and how does this differ from the legacy that the Reformers left us?

3. Look up the following verses and match each one to at least one of the letters in the TULIP acronym. John 10:27-28; Acts 13:48; Matthew 25: 32-33; Romans 9:15; Mark 7:21-23.

SOMETHING EXTRA
A QUICK SUMMARY OF CALVIN'S THELOGY

There is an acronym that is an easy way to remember the different points of Calvin's theology: TULIP

Total Depravity: Every part of humanity is under the influence of sin.

Unconditional Election: God does not choose someone for salvation based on the individual person. We have nothing in us that deserves salvation. We have done nothing that deserves salvation. God chooses to save those that he chooses to save by his own will.

Limited Atonement: Although Christ's death was sufficient to save all mankind, he only died for those that God chose to save. In the Gospel of John, we see that Jesus prayed for all who were given to him, and not for the entire world.

Irresistible Grace: When God calls someone to salvation, they cannot resist. God alone chooses who will believe. All faith is a gift from God.

Perseverance of the Saints: You cannot lose your salvation. Salvation is God's gift so there is nothing that you can do that will get rid of your salvation. God's work of salvation is always completed and this is when the believer reaches heaven.

8
John Knox
(1514—1572)

*John Knox was a Scottish theologian and reformer. He was a
founder of the Presbyterian Church of Scotland.*

Have you ever heard of the word 'hindsight'? It's the
ability of someone to look back at the past and accurately
say, 'That is what they should have done,' or sigh, 'What
were they thinking?' Hindsight is a great deal easier than
foresight. To have foresight you need to be able to predict
what is going to happen. With hindsight you just look at
what has already taken place and make assumptions.

It can be easy to look back at previous centuries and
say with hindsight that they made mistakes, that they
shouldn't have done this or that. However, as people from
the modern age we often believe that we are the ones who
know best. We don't understand what it was really like to
live in the past. We don't appreciate the people who lived
then.

For example, we are rightly critical about the way
women were treated. It would be a disgrace for women

in the twenty-first century to be refused the vote, or to have goods and property confiscated on their marriage. That's what happened then and it would have been better if it hadn't. But men like John Knox are accused of being anti women when they weren't really. The women John criticised were the major monarchs of his lifetime – and they were formidable and fierce. We need to try and see history from his perspective rather than ours.

One particular problem that kept the countries of Scotland and England in shackles was the corruption of the Roman Catholic Church and the absolute power of the monarchies who supported it. John Knox, an ardent supporter of reformation, was exasperated by the trio of women who held a stranglehold of power in the British Isles: Queen Mary of England, Mary of Guise – the queen Regent of Scotland and Mary Queen of Scots, her daughter. These three women did what they could to stand in the way of freedom of worship, preserving their power and the power of the Roman Catholic Church.

His zeal for reformation gave Knox the audacity to take up his pen in 1556 and write against these women of power – *The Monstrous Regimen of Women.* Their actions and beliefs refused Christian liberty to ordinary individuals. They stood in direct conflict with the Word of God. Knox is criticised today for being anti women, when all he was really doing was standing up for ordinary Christians! Knox's writings were eventually published as a pamphlet in 1588.

Where did this firebrand Reformer come from? John had been born in the border town of Haddington in the Scottish region of East Lothian in the year 1514. He was sent to study at the local grammar school before going on to further studies at St. Andrews University. He took on the role of priest and notary and would have made his living in that way until a pastor, George Wishart, opened John's eyes to the truth. John respected George so much that he agreed to become his bodyguard. Eventually, as well as protecting George on his travels, John also started to tutor the young sons of Protestant Lords. They wanted their heirs to be taught by godly men instead of Roman Catholic priests. It was a life that seemed to suit John well. His strength, courage and broadsword were helping Wishart, and his intelligence and ability to teach was building up the next generation. However, as the nation of Scotland changed, so would John's life.

Mary of Guise's persecution of the Protestant Church was on the rise. In December 1545, Wishart was seized on the orders of Archbishop Beaton to be taken to St. Andrews for trial. Knox would have accompanied his friend into captivity, but George persuaded him to stay and continue to teach his students. 'God bless you. One is sufficient for a sacrifice.' On 1st March, 1546, Wishart was burnt at the stake as Archbishop Beaton looked on from a nearby window.

National unrest resulted and over the following months Knox and his pupils travelled from town to town trying to remain out of the grasp of anti-Protestant powers. In May 1546, the bishop who had overseen Wishart's death was himself murdered and the position of power shifted once more in Scotland. St. Andrews was no longer somewhere for Protestants to avoid, but somewhere that they flocked to, a safe haven. It was in St. Andrews that Knox first, reluctantly, became a preacher and pastor. He now had the freedom to proclaim that people should believe in God's Word alone and that salvation is by faith in Christ alone.

However, the political situation in Scotland shifted once again. Mary of Guise and her troops, with the assistance of the king of France, Henry II, set siege to St. Andrews. French galley ships besieged the castle and on the 31st of July, 1547, John Knox and other notable Protestants were taken prisoner. John was forced into a life as a French galley slave where he and others were chained to benches and forced to row under the whip all day. They criss-crossed the oceans enduring terrible conditions.

The Protestant prisoners were also threatened with torture if they did not pay proper respect when the Roman Catholic Mass was performed on the ship. One day, Knox was ordered to show devotion to a picture of the Virgin Mary. When asked, Knox refused to kiss the picture and instead seized it and threw the image into the sea saying, 'Let our Lady now save herself: she is light enough: let her learn to swim.' After that it was decided that the Scottish prisoners should no longer be asked to take part in the Mass. Knox had taken quite a risk, but it had worked out!

In 1549, Knox was released and sought refuge in Protestant England where eventually he was given a congregation at Berwick-upon-Tweed. He also married a woman named Marjory Bowes. John Knox remained in England alongside other famous Reformed Protestants and even preached to the young King Edward VI. But when the young Protestant King died, his successor, Mary Tudor, was an avowed Roman Catholic. One of her first acts as ruler was to restore the Mass in all churches. The nation of England was no longer a safe haven for Protestants and John Knox left the country in 1554.

The following years were mostly spent in Germany and Geneva until the political map changed again and

Elizabeth I took the English throne. Knox decided that it was now indeed time to return to Scotland. However, Scotland was not so free. Mary of Guise declared Knox an outlaw and Knox and other key Protestant supporters refused to give in to her demands. Unrest followed where Protestants attacked or defended depending on your point of view and the forces of the crown did the same. Mary of Guise relented and promised freedom of conscience, but it wasn't long before she asked the King of France to help her once again. John Knox then sought help from the new Protestant Queen of England and the political manoeuvres continued.

It was only after Mary of Guise's death in 1560 that a treaty was signed and all foreign troops, both French and English, were removed from Scottish soil. John Knox could now start to make Scotland a truly Protestant nation. A Scots Confession of Faith was approved and various laws passed which abolished the power of the pope; condemned all religious practice contrary to the Reformed faith and banned the practice of the Mass.

Many reforms became reality – worship was simplified, and importance given to care of the poor and education. The hope was that teaching boys and girls to read would mean that in the future ordinary people would be able to read the Bible for themselves. The population would no longer have to rely on priests to gain access to God's Word. The worship of God would be based around simply reading, preaching and singing from the Word of God.

However, plans for the Church of Scotland to be democratic (giving each congregation the right to choose its own minister for example) did not at first take place. Plans were put before Parliament but were turned down for economic reasons. Then the young Mary, Queen of Scots, returned to take the throne.

Her arrival did nothing to reduce the rumours that Knox was anti women. Mary was young, pretty and manipulative. The abrupt Reformer was nobody's yes man, but then, Queen Mary was no pushover either. She did not comply with the ban on the Mass and when Knox protested about this, Mary summoned him to the palace accusing him of being a rebel. Knox replied that he was willing to accept her rule as long as the people were. Paul the Apostle had been content to live under the authority of Nero so he, Knox, was happy to do the same with her. However, when Mary asked him if subjects had a right to resist their ruler, Knox's reply was quite adamant. 'If a monarch exceeds their lawful limits they can be resisted even by force.'

The interviews between Queen and Reformer continued with Mary accusing him of this, and Knox accusing her of that – and neither really being willing to make any compromise.

When John Knox took issue with Mary's proposed marriage to the son of Philip II of Spain he maybe took a step too far. During their meeting she burst into tears, 'What have you to do with my marriage? What are you within this country?'

To which John astutely replied that he had been born here. That though he was not of noble birth, he had the same rights and duties as any subject to protect his country. And he certainly saw this arranged marriage between the Scottish Queen and a powerful Roman Catholic as dangerous. However, when Mary started to cry again, we see the softer side of this brusque theologian.

'I have never delighted in the weeping of any of God's creatures; yea I can scarcely well abide the tears of my own boys whom my own hand corrects, much less can I rejoice in your Majesty's weeping. Yet I would rather endure your tears than remain silent and betray my country.'

Mary sharply ordered him out of the room. She didn't marry the Spanish prince but still chose unwisely and was imprudent with her relationships. She gave birth to a son, who would in the future be the ruler of both Scotland and England. However, when Mary was implicated in the death of her husband, her country turned against her. She was removed from the throne and eventually imprisoned, before being beheaded for treason by her cousin and fellow monarch, Queen Elizabeth I.

John Knox went the way of all flesh and died on 24th November, 1572. Before his death he gathered some friends to his bed chamber to say some final words. 'In my heart, I never hated the persons of those against whom I thundered God's judgments; I did only hate their sins, and laboured, according to my power, to gain them to Christ.' At his funeral it was said of him, 'Here lies one who never flattered or feared any flesh.'

Today, nobody is certain where Knox's body was buried. A network of roads and car parks cross over the most likely area, but as nobody took care to note or mark this man's last physical resting place, there is little to mark his life or his passing except for his legacy. And it was that which was important in the end; the ideas he represented, the truth of God's Word and the freedom to worship in Spirit and in truth. These became the foundation stones of a nation, a free one.

Scotland's religion became Presbyterian because of him. It didn't happen during his lifetime – far from it – it was 120 years after his death before his cause became a reality.

But with a free education, the liberty to read God's Word and to worship God according to that Word, the nation of Scotland became known in later years as 'The Land of the Book'.

John Knox might ignite negative passions today in some quarters, but the privileges of freedom we have today were hard fought for by him and others like him. We would do well not to forget.

Things to do
1. On a map find the nations of Scotland, England, France and Switzerland.
2. In a dictionary look up the definition of the word 'sacrifice' – how do lives like Wishart's and Knox's demonstrate Christian sacrifice?
3. Look up the following Scriptures: Isaiah 53, 1 Corinthians 15, and John 17. These were the Scriptures that John Knox asked to be read on his deathbed. John 17 being one of the Scripture passages God had used to bring John to faith in Christ.

9
John Welch
(1570—1622)

John Welch was a Scottish Presbyterian leader who was imprisoned for his faith and then exiled to France.

Have you ever heard of the expression 'feet of clay'? It is a phrase used to describe someone who is looked up to but who has made some big mistakes in their life. Having feet of clay means that your hero is not perfect, perhaps far from it.

John Welch had 'feet of clay' because as a young lad he ran away from home to join a band of robbers. He was a criminal but was never charged. John's family was well-off so perhaps their connections got him off the hook. His father was the Laird of Collieston and John was born in Dumfriesshire in the year 1570. As the second son, John would not have inherited the family properties or titles, but his father still had high hopes for him to attend university. Yet, John was willing to throw it all away and become a fugitive from the law. The band of robbers that he joined were called Border Reivers and had plagued the lands of Scotland and England for centuries.

The Border Reivers plundered the communities that straddled the Scottish and English borders. They reached the peak of their powers in the sixteenth and seventeenth centuries. They came from both Scottish and English communities and stole goods and animals whenever they saw the main chance. That often meant stealing from the less powerful and poorer of the land.

When raiding, these bandits would ride their sturdy ponies over the boggy moss while wearing simple shepherd's clothing or a light armour. Sometimes they would carry lances and small shields, or weapons called crossbows, also known as 'latches'. By the time John Welch joined them as a young lad they were probably using pistols in their skirmishes. Every one of them would have secreted a short knife called a dirk somewhere on their person. These pistols and dirks were not just decoration – they would have been used to hurt, maim and even kill. The men that John Welch had joined up with were merciless thugs.

It wasn't long before young John realised that fact. A bandit's life was not as exciting or as romantic as he had at first thought. The reality was a lot different. The weather was wild, the shelters rough, cold and damp. And if the conditions were unpleasant the men he accompanied were even worse. John probably witnessed extreme violence and perhaps experienced it himself. John, like the prodigal son in the Bible, soon wished that he could go home to his father.

However, he only had the rags he stood up in so, decided to stop by his aunt's house first to seek her help in soothing his father's temper. While he was sheltering there, John's father just happened to come and visit his sister. She decided to break the news gently by first asking her brother if he had any news about his son. At that question the older man burst into tears and expressed his fear that the next time he heard about John it would be that he had been hanged as a thief. Quickly, she reassured her brother that this would not be the case and called young John into the room. John begged forgiveness and his father freely gave it. The Laird was relieved to have his son back where he belonged. John Welch was relieved to be out of the clutches of the Border Reivers and back, reconciled, with his family.

He had been a reluctant student before, but now John was determined to put all that behind him. We aren't told specifically about when or how John Welch came to faith, but his life is a strong evidence of the reality that he had come to Christ. Bright enough to attend Edinburgh University, John Welch knuckled down to his studies and passed his exams. He gained a Master of Arts and on 6th March, 1589, he joined the church as a minister in the town of Selkirk. Within the next couple of years he married a young woman named Elizabeth Knox, one of John Knox's daughters, and began a life of preaching the gospel. That was quite a turn around from vagabond to respectable husband and minister of the church. However, in some ways John was still the strong rebellious lad of his past …

On 18th December, 1596, John was preaching in one of the most important pulpits in the land – St. Giles' Cathedral, Edinburgh. He spoke strongly against the immoral behaviour of the king, James VI. John declared that as it was lawful for a son to take charge of his father should he lose his mind, so then it was lawful for the subjects of the land to bind and take charge of the monarch when his behaviour demonstrated that he had gone mad!

That January, John was declared a rebel by the Crown but amazingly enough he was allowed to continue to preach.

John worked and preached in several different areas and then ended up as an assistant pastor in Ayr. His preaching attracted such crowds that they had to build a new church building to accommodate them all. Not only that, John became notorious with the rogues in the area. He wasn't the sort of preacher who just stayed in a library all day. If there was any trouble brewing in the town, and there quite often was, John would fetch his steel helmet and march into the middle of it all. He would never take a weapon with him as it was important to the pastor that the people of his parish understood him to be a peacemaker. After every fight, John would fetch the culprits, force them to become friends and even eat a meal together in public. It didn't take John Welch long to sort out the social disorder in Ayr. The thugs of the area soon quietened down!

There were other bigger problems in the country, however, that John couldn't tackle. King James VI insisted that he was in charge of the church. He did not wish the Scottish church to be democratic or Presbyterian in style. Rather, he intended to appoint bishops to rule the church in his name so that the monarchy could be brought back to absolute instead of limited power. The best way to ensure that this happened was to meddle with the church's government and General Assembly.

There was an agreement that the king attended the General Assembly every year along with all the ministers of the church. It was there that decisions would be made about doctrine, and discipline and other important matters. Even though the king had agreed that the church should have an Assembly every year, and more times if necessary, the king flouted his position of power by frequently delaying those meetings. He even communicated his desire that these meetings be stopped altogether. In 1605, when the king tried to stop the General Assembly once more, the Church of Scotland refused and an Assembly was held in Aberdeen in July. On the 26th of July, John and other ministers of the church were imprisoned in the Castle of Blackness where it was reported they were treated even worse than murderers.

Several months later they were put on trial for high treason and declared guilty. Usually the punishment for this was death, but the king reduced this sentence to exile. John and other ministers of the church who had stood against the king were shipped off to some of the remotest parts of the country. John, though, faired worse as he was put on a ship and sent to another land altogether – France.

As John had never lived in France before, the first thing he had to do was learn the language. It didn't take him long though. In just over three months, John had learned French well enough to be able to preach in the language. Eventually, he became the pastor at Saint-Jean-d'Angely and his French congregation were impressed by how correct he was with his grammar. However, they did notice that whenever he got excited with his preaching, his grammar went out the window. When John realised that this was the case, he asked someone in the congregation to stand up whenever he started to make too many mistakes. His grammar and grasp of French improved over time, so that in a few years John was able to even have a book published.

It must have been difficult to live so far away from home with no prospect of ever returning. However, John was content. His family were with him and he was doing what his heart knew to be God's will. He wrote, 'The fulfilment of my ministry is certainly dearer to me than my life itself. Preaching is my principal desire.'

But it was prayer that fuelled that preaching, as one French friar discovered after seeking shelter at John Welch's home. As the old friar lay in his bed at night, he was kept awake by a quiet whispering. Being of a superstitious nature, the visitor thought that the house must be haunted or worse. However, when speaking to one of the French servants the following day, he found out the truth. The Protestant preacher spent many hours quietly praying in his study. The friar decided to find out the truth of the matter and the next evening snuck out of his room to eavesdrop on John Welch's prayers. While listening to the earnest conversation that John had with his God, the French friar had his own eyes opened to the truth of the gospel. The following morning he told John that he too would become a Protestant.

The problem of persecution was never far away, however. The country of France was Roman Catholic and under a strongly Roman Catholic monarch. Saint-Jean-d'Angely was a fortified town that was besieged by King Louis XIII during the war against the Protestants in 1620. Again we see that John Welch's experience as a Border Reiver in his youth, wasn't completely put to waste. This fierce and formidable preacher soon set about organising the Resistance. However, the strength of the local militia was not enough to withstand the armies of the King of France. After the town surrendered, John was summoned before the king where he was lambasted for preaching in a way that was not acceptable. Welch replied that if the king knew what he was actually preaching, he would come to hear him for himself and instruct others to do so, for what he preached was that there was no one on earth above the king. This cunning answer impressed Louis so much that he decided to allow John to continue preaching and promised to protect him too.

John, however, never forgot his native land and as his health deteriorated there was a deep longing to return to the rolling hills and deep lochs of Scotland, to preach once more to his own people. James VI allowed John and his family to return to England, but he would not consent to the Reformer returning to his homeland of Scotland. When they arrived in London, John's wife, Elizabeth, even went as far as to personally plead with the king to allow her husband to return home. King James said that it would be possible as long as John submitted to the bishops. Elizabeth replied that she would rather receive her husband's decapitated head in her lap than see him give up his beliefs in such a degrading way. The Knox's and the Welch's were made of stern stuff!

The only concession that the king was willing to make was to allow John to preach one last time. His last sermon was delivered in London and he died on 2nd April, 1622, two hours after completing it.

Perhaps we can guess what kind of thoughts John was thinking in his last hours, by looking back at a letter he wrote to one lady, Lilias Graham, in the days before he was banished from Scotland.

'I know that Christ Jesus has prepared a room for me; why may I not then, with boldness in his blood, step into that glory into which my Head and Lord has gone before me ... Who shall condemn the man whom God has justified? Who shall lay anything to the charge of the man for whom Christ has died or rather risen again? ... Whom have I in heaven but him, or who desire I on earth besides him? I hope, O Lord, thou will not let me perish. I desire to be with thee …'

Things to do:

1. Take an atlas and find the town of Leith in Scotland on the east coast and then the nation of France. What route would John Welch have taken to arrive in France from Scotland?

2. Look up the definition of the words 'treason' and 'democracy'. Did you know that the charge of treason still exists today?

3. Look up the following Scripture: Luke 15. What do you see here that reminds you of John Welch?

10

Samuel Rutherford

(1600–1661)

Samuel Rutherford was a Scottish Presbyterian pastor, theologian and author, and one of the Scottish Commissioners to the Westminster Assembly.

If you live in the United Kingdom or Canada you have a parliament. You also have a monarch who is the head of state. However, this monarch does not make all the decisions. People who are voted in by others do that – politicians. If you live in the United States and other nations like that, you don't have a monarch but you do have a constitution and a president. Go back far enough in history and none of these countries that I mentioned had those freedoms. The centuries have indeed brought great changes and great liberty.

Samuel Rutherford, a man who was born in the parish of Nisbet in the borders of Scotland, cherished freedom because it meant freedom to worship the one true God. A passionate preacher, he had a brilliant mind – and if you are one of the young people in the United States who can recite the words of the American constitution, then you owe a lot to him, for a book that he wrote called *Lex Rex* influenced pretty much every man who signed the constitution of the United States into law.

Samuel lived at a complicated time in history, one where human beings made terrible decisions. The 1600s, in Scotland, ended up being one of the bloodiest centuries for Christian martyrs. So where did Samuel Rutherford's journey begin?

Samuel and his brothers went to school in Jedburgh Abbey and Samuel who was very bright went on to graduate from the University of Edinburgh. After gaining his Master of Arts he was eventually appointed as a professor of Latin and literature.

It was some time during the 1620s that Samuel became a Christian. Samuel said that all it took was for Christ to look on him and he was saved. It was direct and straightforward. The rest of his life would not be. During these early days at university Samuel first discovered what it was like to face trouble head on. In those days, if you were a professor, you were not supposed to get married without the permission of the university. A strange custom for us in the twenty-first century, but Samuel Rutherford did get married without the university's consent and as a result he lost his post. It was a bit of a scandal and meant that he had to choose a different career. He went into the preaching ministry. Samuel and his young wife ended up in a little out-of-the-way place called Anwoth, which would become very close to his warm, beating pastor's heart. As it turned out, it took a scandal for Samuel to discover that God had called him to preach.

The church in Anwoth was brand new, so Samuel was its first minister. It was clear that even though he had left the university under a cloud, he was delighted to be working for Christ from the pulpit. 'I have received the commission from the royal and princely Master, my Lord Jesus, to preach Christ to the people.'

It wasn't an easy parish to serve. The congregation was spread over miles of windswept hills. However, Rutherford took his responsibilities seriously and trudged or rode in all weathers in order to nurture his congregation and their souls.

As a pastor he preached with passion, wrote letters of great comfort and wisdom and spent long hours in prayer and personal devotions. Just along from his home in Anwoth there was an avenue of trees where he would frequently head to spend time in private prayer. The locals would see him there and it soon became known as 'Rutherford's Walk'.

The time that he spent in prayer was inspired by a deep love he had for his Saviour and this love inspired a love for others. The letters that he wrote to comfort grieving widows and parents were so precious, that many treasured them and kept them safe so that today we have an amazing record of the words that he wrote to individuals in great need.

Samuel could write in this way because he had experienced great need himself. Throughout his life many of his own children died. Rutherford's young wife also died a painful death, while Rutherford suffered from extreme ill-health. This meant, however, that when the time of persecution came, Samuel had no family to worry about. It was him alone who faced the wrath of men like Thomas Sydserff, a man who hated the Reformation and all it stood for.

Samuel believed that worship of God was so important that you must take the Word of God to be your guide to the worship of God. Other man-made rituals and practices had no place in God's house. The anti-Reform bishops of the church, like Thomas Sydserff, had other ideas and set their sights on Rutherford. As a result, Samuel was kicked out of Anwoth and banished to the city of Aberdeen. For just under two years he was forced to live away from his home and forbidden to preach in public. It almost broke his heart to know that his little church in Anwoth had been left without a pastor to care for their souls, but it was during this time that a lot of Samuel's most cherished letters were written.

It wasn't long before people in Aberdeen started to show an interest in the gospel and this began to annoy the powerful anti-Reform group there. However, Samuel would say warmly, 'I like a rumbling and roaring devil best.' The conflict didn't scare him, instead it gave him confidence that God was at work.

Now, we know for sure that tomorrow comes after today, so change is certain to occur in history. Something was happening at that point in Scotland that would change Rutherford's circumstances quite dramatically.

James VI had died and his son Charles I inherited his throne. Despite the change in monarch there was the same power struggle – where the king desired ultimate power of his nation and the nation's church. Charles I had a strong control of the Church of England which was run by bishops – and he wanted this form of church government to be in Scotland too. However, the land of John Knox had a Presbyterian style of church government. The easiest way to describe this is that it was more democratic. However, Charles I planned to change things and he had bishops and archbishops in place who would support him.

The Scottish Church was urged by Reformers like Rutherford to defend purity of worship and to do all they possibly could to avoid the man-made inventions of the Roman Catholic tradition. This resulted in a very important event in Scottish history – the signing of the National Covenant on 1st March, 1638.

This document was signed by thousands. Some took it so seriously that they even signed it in their own blood. They vowed to defend godly, biblical worship and God's own church. Although Rutherford wasn't actually at the signing of the covenant, because he was still in Aberdeen, he definitely agreed with the document and after it was signed, he was able to return home.

However, others in the church thought that his talents were wasted in Anwoth. The Church of Scotland asked him to take on the role of Professor of Divinity in St. Andrews University. Samuel did not want to do this at first and his congregation certainly didn't want to let him go, but Samuel gave in on the one condition that he be allowed to preach in the city.

When Samuel began his work at St. Andrews it was a troubled era for Scotland and England. Charles I plotted a war against Scotland, but the Scots won. He was also having conflicts within England too. Charles I's own Parliament wanted reform and joined forces with Scotland. The two forces formed the Solemn League and Covenant to seek reformation of the church, not just in Scotland but in England too.

One of the outcomes of this movement for change was the Westminster Assembly. A group of theologians and Members of Parliament gathered together to debate how to reform the church. Samuel Rutherford was asked to join the discussions as a Scottish representative. His contributions were invaluable, especially when devising a document called *The Larger and Shorter Catechism*. Samuel had spent a lot of his own personal time writing a catechism that he had used to teach his congregation in Anwoth the truth of God's Word. A catechism was a commonly used method to teach simple truths, by having people learn a series of questions and answers.

In the year 1644, Samuel also wrote the book that some people see as his greatest work: *Lex Rex: The Law and the Prince*. If you were to pick one particular point that he was making in this book, it would be that kings as well as commoners are under the authority of God and his Word. It was a very popular title and sold a lot. However, by the time it was printed, the conflict in England between Parliament and the king had escalated to such a degree that the country was now in the full throes of civil war. Rutherford's book spoke out against the tyranny of kings, but he was not a supporter of what eventually happened – the execution of Charles I by the Parliamentarian forces.

Samuel returned to Scotland in 1647 and a new conflict. Although Scotland had fought alongside the English Parliament forces, they were now fighting against them and the new interim ruler of England, Oliver Cromwell. History is always complicated.

England was fighting Scotland because Scotland had decided to put Charles I's son, Charles II, on the throne and crowned him King of Scotland, England and Ireland in 1651. Scotland had asked Charles to abide by certain requests, such as keeping Scotland's Church as Presbyterian. The new monarch was more than willing to comply. However, Charles had no plans to keep his word, only his power. When Charles II was eventually enthroned in England, a time of great persecution arrived. Charles II's promises to the Scottish Church were completely forgotten and the Presbyterian Church of Scotland was forced underground with pastors being thrown out of their homes and congregations compelled to meet in the open air. The next thirty years would infamously be called 'The Killing Times' as hundreds of Christians would die for their beliefs.

Samuel Rutherford was summoned to stand before the king on charges of treason – and the only reason that he was saved from martyrdom was that due to ill health he was days away from death himself.

When informed of the King's request, he simply replied, 'I have a summons already from a superior Judge and it is better that I answer my first summons. I now go to be where few kings and great folks come.'

Amongst the last words Rutherford spoke were, 'Glory. Glory dwelleth in Immanuel's Land' and with that he died.

Things to do:
1. On an atlas find the cities of St. Andrews, Edinburgh, Aberdeen and London. In what order did Samuel Rutherford go to these cities?
2. In a dictionary look up the word 'covenant'. Can you think of three other words that you might use instead of covenant that mean the same thing or something similar?
3. Look up the following verses about covenants that God has made in the Bible: Genesis 9:12-13; Exodus 2:24; Psalm 89:28; Matthew 26:28; Hebrews 7:22.

11
John Owen
(1616–1683)

John Owen was an English nonconformist church leader, theologian, and academic.

Are you ever compared to someone else? Someone might say that you look like a relative or that you remind them of a friend. Imagine if people compared you to someone famous? A successful soldier and national leader might be compared to Julius Caesar or Winston Churchill. Famous writers, even today, still get compared to Charles Dickens. John Owen is described by some people as the English John Calvin because, with this particular hero, we have an example of someone whose heroic deeds are through his thoughts and his pen.

Did you know that you can be a hero in a library just as much as on a battlefield? You can be a triumph as you lift up a pen or a spade – it doesn't have to be a sword. You can change the world while wearing a boiler suit – you don't necessarily need to be dressed like 007 or the King of Spain.

In the Kingdom of God it doesn't matter what you look like as long as what you do is to the glory of God. As you go on through life making decisions and choices, keep that in mind. You may be called on to do great things that people are astonished at. If so, give the glory to God. You will more than likely be asked to do ordinary things – definitely do these to the glory of God.

John Owen's life fits into the spade and boiler suit style of Christian life. His life probably won't be made into a dramatic Hollywood film, but if you are going to have a realistic view of the church and its story, you should find out about this man of God.

To start off, he was born in the year that William Shakespeare died, 1616. Four years after his birth, the Pilgrim Fathers set sail for the new world. This was quite a time to be alive in history. Looking back we can see that things happened during this time that changed the world. John Owen's life and work would change the church, building it up for the future with pen and ink. Where did his life begin? It wasn't a great cathedral city but a little village in Oxfordshire named Stadhampton. John's backwoods childhood, however, must have had some fond memories as he would return there off and on throughout his life. Though there aren't many other physical details about his early childhood, it is possible to make some educated guesses about one or two things.

John would remember in his own writings the joy of bedtime stories that would soothe a child to sleep. He also wrote later in his life that, 'When a child is abused abroad in the street by strangers he runs with speed to the bosom of his father and is comforted.'[1] Perhaps we are reading

---

1. Owen Works 2:38. *The Works of John Owen*, Wentworth Press, 2016.

here some early memories of John's loving family life. A father's protection was a great thing to have during the 1600s. Although the Civil War was a few years away, there was still unrest and strong disagreement within the land regarding politics and religion. Whatever causes unrest in the adult world makes its way into the playground. John's godly upbringing would have brought ridicule on John and his siblings. Name-calling would not have been uncommon. Originally, the name Puritan would have been a term of abuse so the young John may very well have run home in tears at some of the horrid things his classmates said to his face. Perhaps you can identify with that – cruel words can hurt as much as cruel actions.[2]

When he was only twelve years old, John Owen went to study at Queen's College, Oxford where he gained a Master of Arts. He was a committed and intelligent student, often disciplining himself to only four hours of sleep a night, as well as enjoying some vigorous physical exercise called 'throwing the bar'. He thought very little about his need of salvation, however, and if his thoughts went to the church at all, it was purely because he had ambitions to make a great career there. This might have happened as he was clever enough and had been admitted to a leadership role, so he could have gone on to other things. John Owen soon found, though, that his principles were in direct conflict with the practices of the church. John had to make a decision. Could he give up his plans and stand up for what he knew to be biblical truth?

The problem was that the University of Oxford had a new chancellor, William Laud, whose aim was to bring back pre-Reformation practices to the university. Men like

2. Owen Works 8:177; 197; 14:153. *The Works of John Owen*: Wentworth Press, 2016.

Laud cared more about man-made traditions than biblical doctrine and beliefs. It was more important to them that you wore the right robes than preached the truth of the Bible.

William Laud wanted laws or statutes to be adopted, which meant that the church would be controlled by the king and men appointed by him. Those men wanted to control the worship of God by insisting that preachers wore certain clothes and used things like incense, bells and prayer books during church services. The Puritans insisted that the worship of God must be simple and with nothing in it that was not directly mentioned in God's Word.

John was a Puritan at heart so had to leave all his plans for a university career behind him. During those days, unlike today, the universities were part of the church. So, John knew that he could not hope to rise up through the ranks of the church because of his beliefs. What he believed in went against what powerful men in the church believed, even the king. Because of his beliefs John could now no longer even inherit his wealthy uncle's fortune. John's uncle cut his nephew off from any support when it was clear that the young man identified with the Puritans and that he did not support the king.

So, John left the university because he had to make a stand for the truth. Yet, he still had many doubts and questions about what that truth actually meant. However, even in the middle of all these problems and struggles John didn't starve, as God provided for him – guiding him towards people who would employ him as their chaplain or as a tutor to their sons.

Then one morning, after years of struggling with his doubts and fears, John Owen went to hear a famous preacher. Instead of the famous preacher, though, he found himself listening to a complete stranger from the country. This unknown man read out Matthew 8:26: 'Why are ye so fearful , O ye of little faith?' Something about these words from the Bible captured John's attention and he prayed to God that somehow this minister would speak to his heart. Did God hear his prayer? Of course he did. Every question that John had was answered by this unknown stranger. John had entered the church that day with great fears and doubts, but he left with great peace.

What was the name of this unknown country preacher? John never found out. Despite all his best efforts, John was never able to discover the name of the man who had brought him to trust in Jesus Christ for salvation.

However, the peace he obtained through this man's sermon was the foundation of everything he did from then on. It would bring him through great troubles. His wife, Mary, would give birth to eleven children, but ten of them would die before they reached adulthood. He would also face persecution. John's struggles in life went up and down along with the nation's politics. He was a Puritan as far as his faith was concerned, but when it came to politics he would have preferred tolerance of other points of view. After Charles I was beheaded by Parliament, John was asked to make it clear what side he supported – Parliament or the King. John refused. John did go on to be a friend and confidant of the Parliamentary leader Oliver Cromwell, but he also stood against him when Cromwell announced his plans to crown himself as king.

When Cromwell died and Charles II came to power, the position of the Puritans and John Owen changed completely. The Act of Uniformity put 2,000 Puritans out of their pulpits in the year 1662.

What we have as John Owen's lasting legacy are books – the books that he wrote. Some of them are very long – over 600 pages. Some of them were shorter, like a little book called *The Mortification of Sin*[3]. Mortification is a word we don't use much today, but it means humiliation or putting to death. John Owen was writing about how we need to put sin in its place, kick it out of our lives, focus on giving God the glory. Another word for this is holiness. John Owen said, 'Be killing sin or it will be killing you.'[4]

'Fill your affections with the Cross of Christ so that there will be no room for sin'.[5]

He wrote how he hoped that the chief design of his life would be holiness and that this would be promoted in his own heart and in the hearts and ways of others, to the glory of God, 'so that the gospel of our Lord and Saviour Jesus Christ may be adorned in all things.'

Even though his main legacy is his writing, it would be wrong to think of him just as someone who hid behind a desk. He was a passionate preacher and a pastor – he loved the people. One of his friends, Richard Baxter, described him as a 'great do-er'. He was involved with the church and with politicians, he worked alongside soldiers and the military leaders of his day. He had a great longing to teach children and young people the truth of God's Word.

---

3. Owen, John, *The Mortification of Sin*, Christian Focus Publications, 2012.
4. Owen, John, *On the Nature, Power, Deceit and Prevalence of Indwelling Sin in Believers*, Kindle edition, Amazon.
5. Owen, John, *On the Nature, Power, Deceit and Prevalence of Indwelling Sin in Believers*, Kindle edition, Amazon.

Today we find the real John Owen through the words that he left behind. One of the last books that he wrote was a commentary on the book of Hebrews.

'We are never nearer Christ than when we find ourselves lost in a holy amazement at his unspeakable love.'[6]

One of the last things he wrote was a letter in which he clearly showed where his great passion was: 'I am going to him whom my soul hath loved, or rather hath loved me with an everlasting love ... I am leaving the ship of the church in a great storm, but while the great Pilot is in it the loss of a poor under-rower will be inconsiderable.'

Owen died on 24th August, 1683, at sixty-seven years of age. He was buried on 4th September in Bunhill Fields, London.

Things to do:
1. Find a map of England and look for the city of London and Oxford. If you can find a map of London, can you find Bunhill Fields there? Today Bunhill Fields can be found in the London borough of Islington.
2. In a dictionary find the definition of the word 'mortification' and then 'humility' and 'holiness'. Three words that sum up John Owen.
3. In the Bible read Matthew 8. In this chapter what does Jesus show his power over as well as the wind and the waves?

---

6. Owen, John, *An Exposition of the Epistle to the Hebrews,* Kindle edition, Amazon.

BUILDING ON
THE REFORMERS

12
William Wilberforce
(1759—1833)

William Wilberforce was a British politician and leader of the movement to abolish the slave trade.

Being involved in politics and activism is not unusual today. In our world we hear a lot about young people campaigning for the rights of others. You might, for instance, have a passion for the environment. To support that cause you are perhaps trying to reduce your use of plastic or energy. You might be concerned about your carbon footprint. Perhaps you follow different charities such as Barnabus Fund in order to support Christians around the world who are facing persecution. There are lots of problems in our society that need the impact of Christ. William Wilberforce is a Christian remembered primarily for campaigning against slavery, something that is still a problem in our world today.

In the modern world slavery raises its head in places like sweat shops where whole families are forced to work long hours for very little pay. In protest, some people refuse to purchase clothes unless it can be proven that they were made in ethical ways.

In previous centuries slaves were often captured during combat, or sold into slavery in order to pay debts. Then something changed which meant that a lot of the world's slaves came from one continent – Africa. This meant that most of the slaves in the time of William Wilberforce had the same skin colour – a skin colour that people at that time called black. Unjustly, people of this colour became a commodity and were at the centre of one of this planet's largest trades that criss-crossed the oceans.

Britain became involved in the slave trade in the sixteenth century. That nation's goods were brought to Africa in order to buy slaves, and these slaves were then transported to British colonies in the West Indies where they were put to work on the sugar, tobacco and cotton plantations. The product that was produced by the labour of these men, women and children was then shipped back to Britain. The slave trade represented a large part of Great Britain's foreign income. Britain's involvement in the slave trade meant that they supplied other countries with slaves and goods as well. At its peak, British slave ships carried 40,000 slaves across the Atlantic in horrific conditions. It is said that over a 400-year period, 12.8 million Africans were transported into slavery of which 1.4 million died during the voyage.

This was the system that William Wilberforce committed his life to abolishing.

So, let's find out a bit about where this reforming politician began his life.

William was born in 1759, in the town of Hull which is in Yorkshire in the north of England. Today, in Hull, there is a house called Wilberforce House which was the family home. Outside it there is a statue in William's honour. Imagine having a statue outside your flat or house years after you had lived there. In the 1700s when Wilberforce's parents looked after their little son, they perhaps had high hopes for him, but would never have imagined that one day there would be a statue of their son on the pavement. The Wilberforces were, however, quite well off. William's grandfather had been elected twice as the Mayor of Hull so the family had political connections.

As a lad, William's health was not great and he was described as being small and sickly. He didn't have good eyesight either. When he was quite young William's father died, which changed William's life dramatically. His mother wasn't coping, so she decided to send William to her brother's home. When he was only nine years old, young William Wilberforce went to live with his uncle and aunt in London. From there he was sent to boarding school but would return to his uncle and aunt's for his holidays and became very fond of them. He also became interested in their nonconformist religious beliefs. His uncle and aunt took him to hear the preaching of John Newton, the ex-slave ship captain, and as young lad Wilberforce held him in great esteem.

His Aunt Hannah was a strong evangelical Christian. Both she and her husband were 'nonconformist'. In England, at that time, this meant that you didn't believe in following the strict traditions of the established Anglican Church.

When William's mother heard that her son was being influenced by his uncle and aunt in this way, she immediately took him home, insisting that he be educated by a staunch Church of England school. William was upset at first, but as he settled into his new school he forgot his aunt's religious beliefs and began to spend his free time in things like theatre-going, dancing and gambling.

When he was seventeen years old, Wilberforce went to study at Cambridge University. He had been left a sizeable legacy which meant he had no financial concerns whatsoever. Instead of worrying about his exams or his future, William threw himself into a flamboyant social life of playing cards and drinking. Wilberforce was the heart of any social gathering or party and as a result became quite the popular man about town. He made a lot of friends, one of whom would become a future British prime minister: William Pitt. Everything was going well for Wilberforce and, even though he didn't really devote himself to studies, he still managed to pass his exams!

He decided that a life in politics was the perfect job for him and in 1780 William Wilberforce was elected as a Member of Parliament for his hometown of Hull. We're used to people joining a political party before they become a Member of Parliament, but William didn't want to belong to a particular group and joined Parliament as an independent candidate. William would support whichever side in Parliament that he thought had the best arguments. At that time there were two groups struggling for overall power in government, one was called the Whigs and the other was called the Tories. William would vote with one group and then later on vote with the other. He wasn't that tall, or physically imposing but he made up for it in other ways. When he sang he had a great voice. The Prince of Wales said he would travel almost anywhere to hear Wilberforce sing. And then when he spoke, he was even more powerful. At one point, in Wilberforce's life, the famous diarist James Boswell wrote that when Wilberfoce spoke in Parliament: 'I saw what seemed a mere shrimp … but as I listened, he grew, and grew, until the shrimp became a whale.' Wilberforce did all this while still enjoying parties and gambling and having a grand old time.

He didn't let his politics get in the way of his personal pastimes and enjoyments. In 1784, he went on a tour of Europe with his mother, his sister and a friend named Isaac Milner. The two young men decided to read a book together on their travels called *The Rise and Progress of Religion in the Soul*. It was written by a man called Philip Doddridge who was a nonconformist. Something in this book reignited the passion and interest that William had once had for the Christian faith while staying with his uncle and aunt. However, this time it became more than just an interest.

William began to eagerly read the Bible and pray. He regretted deeply the sins of his past and made a commitment that, in the future, he would live his life for God. The pastimes of drinking and gambling were discarded and in their place came a passion for the way of God and for the people God had created. William knew, though, that this new found faith of his would cause him problems. Evangelical Christians were looked down on in high society and William knew it would be difficult to continue in politics. There was one man of his acquaintance who could give him good advice. William went to visit a voice from his past, the Anglican evangelical minister John Newton. Newton's advice was to remain in politics. This elderly minister clearly saw the need to have Christians in every sphere of life, particularly where the laws and decisions were made. John Newton, an ex-slave ship captain, wanted men like Wilberforce in positions of power in order to stand up against the slave trade.

'It is hoped and believed that the Lord has raised you up for the good of his church and for the good of the nation.'

One day while having dinner with a friend, William met James Ramsay. This man had been a ship's surgeon and had also worked on some of the Caribbean plantations in his role as a medic. He had seen first-hand the terrible conditions that the slaves were kept in on board the ships and how they were treated by their masters. On returning to England, Ramsay had met with other people equally as horrified as he. People like Thomas Clarkson and Hannah More encouraged Ramsay to write about what he had seen. Meeting Ramsay was one of the first times that Wilberforce would interact with the anti-slavery movement. He was sympathetic to their cause – but they wanted more.

On 13th March, 1787 William was invited to a dinner party. During this meal William was asked to bring the abolition of the slave trade before Parliament. William still had his doubts though and it wasn't until a conversation with his old friend Pitt that Wilberforce finally committed himself to the struggle of abolishing slavery. Sitting underneath an oak tree, William Wilberforce decided that he could not ignore the slave trade any longer and that if he didn't do something now he could possibly lose the opportunity for ever.

'God Almighty has set before me two great objects: the suppression of the slave trade and the reformation of morality.'

As well as the fight against slavery William championed many other causes. As a Christian he believed in the importance of relieving the suffering of others and of God's creation. Here is a list of some of the issues he was passionate about: chimney sweeps, single mothers, orphans, poverty and the prevention of cruelty to animals.

On 22nd May, 1787, the 'Society for Effecting the Abolition of the Slave Trade' was formed with the aim of campaigning against the slave trade and not just slavery itself. The abolitionists believed that once the trade itself was destroyed, slavery would soon follow.

The Society travelled the length and breadth of the country spreading its message. Innovative techniques were used to get across their ideas: pamphlets, public meetings, boycotts. They designed their own logo and even reached out to other countries such as Spain, Denmark, Holland and the United States. Many people decided to stop taking sugar in their tea in protest at the slaves being used on the sugar plantations.

Hundreds of thousands of people signed petitions opposing the slave trade. This was the first human rights campaign in history where men and women from different backgrounds and social classes joined forces to fight injustice.

Due to ill health William could not introduce the preparatory motion against slavery, so Pitt did it in his absence. The campaign against slavery in Parliament had begun.

It would be a long struggle. Wilberforce and other abolitionists would find themselves pitted against many who saw slavery as a right, and of great economic importance to the British Empire.

Many who supported slavery claimed that slaves were lesser human beings and that they actually benefited from being slaves. The abolitionists believed that Africans had the same abilities and rights as any other human being.

It wasn't until 23rd February, 1807, that the abolition bill became law. It was carried by 283 votes to 16. The Slave Trade Act received royal assent on 25th March, 1807.

However, this wasn't the end of slavery itself. William still campaigned against that, but his health deteriorated to the extent that he eventually gave up his seat in Parliament.

He gave his last anti-slavery speech in April 1833 and one month later a bill was introduced to Parliament for the abolition of slavery itself. On 26th July, 1833, Wilberforce heard the bill was guaranteed to be passed. From August 1834, slavery would be illegal in most of the British Empire. The following day, however, William Wilberforce died. One month later, the House of Lords passed the Slavery Abolition Act. Approximately 800,000 Africans were freed.

William Wilberforce was buried at Westminster Abbey in London beside his friend William Pitt.

Things to do:

1. On a map of the world trace the route that the British slave trade ships would have taken from the United Kingdom to Zanzibar in Africa to the Caribbean island of Jamaica and then back to Bristol in England. This is referred to as a triangular trade system – can you see why?

2. In a dictionary look up the word 'slavery'. Find out about the Christian, Oluadah Equiano, who was a slave originally from Nigeria.

3. Look up the following Scripture verses: Galatians 3:28; Ephesians 6:9; John 8:34; Proverbs 22:16.

13
Pastor Hsi

(1836–1896)

Pastor Hsi also known as Xi Shengmo was a Chinese Christian leader.

Do you have more than one name? Perhaps you have a nickname. Perhaps you have people in your family who have changed their names over their lifetimes. Quite often women change their last name after their marriage. Some of my Asian friends, if they move to the U.S. or the U.K., adopt a more English sounding name because their new American or British friends find Chinese names too hard to pronounce. Our next Christian hero has several names, the one he was born with, the one he chose and then the one he was given because of what he did.

He was born with the first name: Xi Zizh.

He changed this to Shengmo when he became a Christian because it means 'Conqueror of Demons.

We now know him as Pastor Hsi because after becoming a Christian, the changes didn't stop there. His life had a purpose which was to preach the gospel to the people of

China – a vast nation which for many centuries had never heard the truth of God's Word.

So where did Hsi's life begin? Near the city of Pingyang there lived a family of scholars – the grandfather was a scholar, the father was a scholar and the sons would be also. Hsi was the fourth son in his family and joyfully received by both his parents, for to have sons was seen as a great blessing in Chinese culture. They would provide for their parents when they reached maturity and having four meant that at least one of them was sure to survive into your old age.

We might think it strange today for a family to be so enthusiastic about having sons rather than daughters. On the internet we see gender reveal parties where people cheer at having either pink or blue glitter exploding out of a firework. In the West these days, people usually don't mind if they have a boy or a girl, but it wasn't always the case. In the past, western cultures also showed a bias towards having sons rather than daughters. In previous centuries, families hoped for boys as it meant they would provide for the family's future – girls would marry into other families. So, in China during the 1830s families were very keen to have male heirs.

China was, and still is, a different culture to the West. Its history goes back many centuries with different ruling families called dynasties. The Ming dynasty lasted until the middle of the 1600s and then it was the turn of the Qing dynasty which lasted from 1644 till 1912. At its peak this dynasty ruled over one third of the earth's population with the largest economy in the world. However, by the nineteenth century it was under threat from the West. China was defeated by the British Empire in the First Opium War in 1840. Opium was a substance that, up until that point, had not been consumed much in the Far East as it was recognised by Chinese powers as a dangerous narcotic. It was addictive and its abuse destroyed people's health. It was used widely in other countries for pain relief, but as soon as people started to use it they couldn't stop. They just had to have more. That was the beginning of a slippery slope into addiction. Because of this there was a ban in China against its use. However, opium was a product that the British Empire traded in – it was one of their sources of wealth. Britain saw China as a valuable source of revenue for sales of opium and after defeating China with their superior naval ships they gained territory and trading rights for the drug. This was the beginning of what would be a plague of addiction within the country – a plague that would eventually have a solemn impact on the life of Hsi and his family.

Hsi began his life with great promise. He went to university and was a bright and intelligent young man who had lots of questions rattling around inside his mind. So many of his questions were ones that he could not get answers to, however. As a young boy Hsi would visit the local Buddhist temple where the priests offered incense and worshipped idols. However, this gave the young Hsi no hope or any answers to the questions that plagued him. The young student could see no use for life, for living in this world, for amassing the riches and fame that his family encouraged him towards.

His marriage was arranged for him by his parents as was the custom of his people and, when his father passed away, Hsi found himself well provided for with house and lands and a scholarly career ahead. Surely he had all he needed? Yet, something was missing. Not even gaining a reputation as a just leader soothed his anxiety.

With all of these advantages you would think that Hsi would finally be content and at rest – but he was not. His young wife passed away and there were no children to gladden his heart. Questions and doubts still haunted him.

Hsi had for his whole life been a student of a belief called Confucianism – but it had given him none of the answers he sought after. He tried other beliefs but with no joy. 'I am forlorn, as one who has no home … I am enveloped in darkness … I toss about as if on the sea. I float to and fro as though I were never to rest.'

After his second marriage Hsi looked into the belief of Taoism which promised an immortal life, but not long after he began this religion Hsi's health took a turn for the worse. He could see that this religion was not the answer either in his desperate search for God. His illness increased so much that friends suggested to him that he might find some relief if he tried opium. It was terrible advice, but Hsi didn't realise how terrible until it was too late. It may have given him some relief at first, but the more he smoked the worse his sufferings became. He no longer had any appetite and found it difficult to sleep. Nothing mattered to him any more but the consumption of opium. His health became so poor that his family truly expected him to die any day and they actually began to dress his body for burial. Hsi passed in and out of consciousness and was perhaps moments away from death when he heard a voice with such authority shout at him, 'Go back! Go back!' Hsi realised that he had no choice and had to obey the voice. In later years Hsi believed that this had indeed been the voice of God.

His opium addiction did more than destroy his health, the family finances were diminished as was the promise of his once brilliant career. Opium was like a plague and like any other infection it had spread rapidly throughout the country. Most of the local farms in Hsi's area now produced poppies, the plant from which opium is derived. They stopped producing other crops that would actually feed people. When the drought came, famine followed soon after and if it had not been for his family farm's store of grain, Hsi would also have been amongst the many who perished from starvation during that time. As it turned out, his family survived while still managing to supply Hsi with enough opium to feed his addiction. When Hsi had been an addict for about ten years or more, news came to the area that two foreigners had arrived in Pingyang – two English men.

Now, understandably, because of the previous conflict and the devastating impact of opium on the country, many, like Hsi, were suspicious of people who came from Britain. When he heard that they were Christian missionaries, this did nothing to reassure him. He was intrigued, though, when he heard that the men dressed like Chinese men, that they had learned his language and were apparently fixed on staying for good. Even so, Hsi had no desire to see these men or speak to them. Hsi had no interest in this new religion – there were enough religions already, who needed a new one! Apparently these men were talking about worshipping the one true God who could answer everyone's prayers. Hsi thought that was ridiculous – everyone knew that God was too far away to be spoken to in that manner. Even the local mandarin ruler was too busy to attend to all the local problems – how could God attend to everyone's prayers? Hsi had no idea about the real power of an omnipotent God! All he had were his doubts about the religions and faiths of his own people. No faith that he had looked at so far had given him any peace.

However, as it turned out, peace was not that far away as God had plans for Hsi to meet a missionary named David Hill.

The missionaries, when they arrived at Pingyang, surprised everyone with their good deeds and care for the needy. They also impressed people with their good living – there was no sign of alcohol abuse or loose living. However, even though the missionaries made such a good impression, things weren't going as well as they had hoped. David Hill realised that to make an impact on the local population they first had to make an impact on the educated scholars. Once men like those were opened up to the good news of Jesus Christ then the message would spread to other levels of society. But how to reach these educated men? Between them, the missionaries came up with the idea of devising an essay competition for which the winner would gain a substantial prize. They would hand out a list of topics all of which would be on Christian themes. Only scholars could compete and the essay competition itself would encourage the men to think about Christianity for themselves. If they ran the competition in early autumn it would coincide with the scholarly examinations and there would be thousands of scholarly men in the city anyway. Thousands of Christian books and tracts were handed out to the competitors and one of those competitors ended up being Hsi. His brothers had heard of the competition and persuaded him to compete. 'You are after all the cleverest out of all of us – you are bound to walk away with one of the prizes.' Hsi reluctantly agreed.

Eventually, David Hill received back 120 different essays to read, three of which were from Hsi. He had also been persuaded by his brothers to write essays on their behalf! Hsi won three different prizes including the overall first prize. Reluctantly, Hsi agreed to meet with the missionary to accept his prize. When he arrived at the missionary's house he was nervous of these 'foreign devils'. Certain there must be something sinister about them. He even refused to drink the tea that was offered by the house servant. However, when David Hill entered the room Hsi's many prejudices melted away in a moment – this was no devil. David was polite and pleasant looking, kind and very complimentary of Hsi's essay. After accepting the prize money, David let Hsi depart with no other questions or discussion. Again Hsi was somewhat surprised – he had been sure the missionary would demand that he became a Christian. But David had said nothing at all.

Hsi went home. David waited and then a few days later he sent Hsi a message. 'I have a favour to ask of you Mr. Hsi as I am in great need of some scholarly assistance. Will you come and help me in my work? I need someone to help me write some essays. If you could come and stay with me for some time in order to assist me in this work, I would be very grateful.'

Hsi was secretly rather proud to be asked for help by the foreign missionary and agreed to come and help him. From the beginning of his time with David, Hsi not only heard the gospel but saw it in action. The home life of the missionary had a great impact on Hsi. He saw the missionary at his reading, writing, preaching, prayer, eating, housework and socialising. David wisely gave Hsi his space – allowing him to observe the life of a Christian home. The missionary didn't force Christianity on his guest but waited for God's timing. He just made sure to leave a book sitting on a table, or a tract near a chair – anyplace that Hsi might happen upon it, then pick it up to read. Eventually, this tactic worked. The Chinese scholar began to realise that Jesus Christ was not just an ordinary man but God himself, a mighty Saviour. However, instead of losing anxiety over his sin, it increased, but this was part of God's plan. Hsi's anxieties finally sent

Hsi to his knees in prayer – seeking salvation from its only true source, Christ. Hsi's heart rejoiced at the truth of God's Word, 'He loved me and gave himself for me.' With a flood of tears Hsi yielded himself to his Redeemer – the one who had died on the cross for his sins.

With this new faith in Christ, Hsi's life was completely changed, but he still suffered from his opium addiction. David knew that this was an issue that neither of them could ignore. 'I deeply regret to see the hold that opium has over you,' David said to Hsi. It was clear that the new Christian would not be able to be an example to others while he was still under the control of the drug.

Hsi agreed that coming off the drug was what his new Lord and Saviour required of him. It was no easy task and Hsi suffered greatly with withdrawal symptoms. The whole process was exhausting, painful and agonizing, but Hsi was determined never to go back to opium. Throughout the whole ordeal Hsi constantly threw himself on the Lord in prayer. The more he suffered the more he realised it wasn't just a physical battle he was involved in but a spiritual one. The devil was doing all he could to keep Hsi captured by opium. After many days of anguish, Hsi's attention was grasped by some words in Scripture that referred to the Holy Spirit as 'Comforter'. The mighty power given to strengthen men. He cried out to God for the power of his Holy Spirit, the one who could make impossible things possible, overcoming all the power of the enemy. Suddenly the anguish ceased and his heart was flooded with peace. God 'did what man and medicine could not do and my whole body was perfectly at rest.'

From that moment on, for the rest of his life, Hsi realised that the only power that can truly deliver is Christ.

'Don't lean on man but trust only in God.'

Hsi found himself called to a life of service to the one true God and the first place that he knew he had to preach in was his own village and to his own family. They thought he had been bewitched, the change in his life was so dramatic. Hsi decided that now would be a good time to mark this miraculous change by changing his name to 'Conqueror of Demons'. Everyone could see that there had been a change – and the ones who noticed it most were the women he lived with. His wife had never seen him so bright and loving. Before he had become a Christian, he had not cared to teach them anything – it was not the Confucian way to teach women. Now, Hsi longed for all men and women to possess the truth of the gospel.

Towards the end of 1894, Hsi wrote a letter that sums up the direction his life took: 'During the fifteen years that have elapsed since I first believed in the Lord Jesus, I have sometimes been engaged in leading the Christians in farming; sometimes in helping to cook in the kitchen … sometimes in assisting with the manufacture of our medicines; sometimes even in domestic work, as well as in travelling from province to province arranging for the Refugees, preaching and healing diseases or assisting to govern the affairs of the Church. I humbly beg all the foreign missionaries and native pastors to pray for me, …. That I may give myself unremittingly to prayer and the preaching of the gospel. This is what my heart truly longs for.'

Pastor Hsi's life was given to the service of God. Then in the year 1896, on a February morning, he passed into the presence of his Lord and Saviour. To many he was held in much affection and his wife deeply mourned him, but she was amongst one of the people who had accepted Jesus Christ through Hsi's ministry and was able to say, 'I think of Jesus – and he is enough.'

Things to do:
1. On a map look at the size of China in relation to other countries of the world. How does the size of this country compare to the country you live in?
2. In a dictionary look up the definition of the word 'worship'.
3. In the Bible look up these Scripture verses: John 4:24; Deuteronomy 11:16; Psalm 97:7; Luke 4:8; Romans 12:1; Hebrews 12:28. What do these verses teach us about who to worship and how?

SOMETHING EXTRA

Much has happened in the land of China since the death of Pastor Hsi. Not long after his passing, the Boxer Rebellion began. This was an anti-imperialist and anti-Christian rebellion that happened at the beginning of the twentieth century and resulted in the massacre of many missionaries and Chinese Christians. A republic of China was declared on 1st January, 1912. Then in 1949 the People's Republic of China was formed by the Chinese Communist Party. Since then, the persecution of Christians has escalated in that land but so has the advance of the gospel. The Church in China now numbers in excess of 100 million people. Considering that the first version of the Bible available in Chinese was printed in 1807, this is amazing. China's Christians already outnumber American Christians, as well as Chinese Communist Party members, yet still comprise less than 20% of China's 1.4 billion people.

14

Charles Spurgeon

(1834—1892)

Charles Haddon Spurgeon was an English Baptist preacher and writer, often referred to as the 'Prince of Preachers'.

Charles Haddon Spurgeon was born on 19th June, in the year 1834, in Kelvedon, Essex. He was the first of seventeen children that would be born to John and Eliza Spurgeon and he would go on to be one of the most prolific Christian writers and preachers of the Victorian age.

The Victorian age was the period of history during which Queen Victoria was on the throne, during the years of 1837—1901. It was an era of great advancements – a vibrant and perhaps controversial time to be alive. In 1834 Michael Farraday published the results of his experiments with electricity and today we have a world of light at the turn of a switch. However, in the year of Spurgeon's birth we see other changes that demonstrate the darker side of Victorian life. Slavery was brought to an end through the Slavery Abolition Act that was introduced in 1833. The Poor Law Amendment Act meant that no able-bodied man could receive monetary assistance from the state unless he was willing to enter a poor house. The Chimney Sweeps Act of 1834 was introduced to stop the ill-treatment of young children who were forced to climb up chimneys in order to clean them. This Act banned all employment of children under the age of ten as chimney sweeps. Acts of legislation, like these, demonstrate that the Victorian era had much poverty and injustice, as well as many people willing to fight against them.

This was the world that Charles Spurgeon was born into. It was a world that needed help and hope. The young boy born in 1834, would eventually share with the world where that hope could be found but first he had to find it himself.

On 6th January, 1850 Charles Spurgeon was walking to church, but he ended up going to a different church than the one he had planned to go to. A bitter blizzard forced him into the first church building that he could find. It was called the Primitive Methodist Chapel. When Charles began to listen to the preacher that day, he wasn't impressed – not at all. He thought he was 'stupid' and as for the man's pronunciation, well, he was pretty sloppy in the young teenager's opinion. However, it was from the lips of this stumbling country parson that Charles heard the words that turned him to Christ.

The preacher's text that day was Isaiah 45:22 – 'Look unto me, and be ye saved, all the ends of the earth, for I am God, and there is none else.' It was as if the preacher was speaking directly to him and him alone. And suddenly he was – he turned to Charles and said to him, 'Young man you look very miserable!'

Charles had to admit to himself that he was.

The preacher continued, 'and you always will be miserable – miserable in life, and miserable in death, if you don't obey my text; but if you obey now, this moment, you will be saved. Young man, look to Jesus Christ. Look! Look! Look! You have nothin' to do but to look and live.'

Later, Spurgeon would say of this experience, 'Simply by looking to Jesus, I had been delivered from despair, and I was brought into such a joyous state of mind that, when they saw me at home, they said to me, "Something wonderful has happened to you" and I was eager to tell them all about it …'

Then, on the 3rd of May, in the River Lark, at Isleham Charles was baptised. It wasn't long before he became a Sunday School teacher and then he preached his first sermon in a little cottage in the village of Teversham. On this day, Charles became a preacher – something that would be his purpose for the rest of his life. From the very beginning of his ministry, Charles' God-given gifts were obvious to many. His abilities to preach and share the gospel meant that, within a year of his baptism, he was given the pastorate of a small Baptist church in Cambridgeshire. In the same year he also wrote his first gospel tract.

By the time he was nineteen years old, Charles was called to take over the ministry at London's biggest Baptist congregation: New Park Street in Southwark. His preaching soon became famous and many people flocked to hear him. His sermons were also published so that people who were not there could read the same message for themselves.

In 1856, Spurgeon married a young woman named Susannah and in 1857 they had twin sons. By the time Charles was twenty-two years old he was already the most popular preacher of his day.

The congregation eventually outgrew the space available at New Park Street and Spurgeon had to give his sermons in the Surrey Music Hall. A typical audience for Charles at that time would have been around 10,000 people, but one time that he preached at the Surrey Music Hall, tragedy struck.

His fame came with problems. The media of the day did not like him. Some resented the dramatic way he preached and called him the 'preaching buffoon'. However, his passion and way with words attracted the ordinary people – Spurgeon brought the Bible to life. It may have been his popularity and the resulting dislike from certain quarters that caused the terrible accident at the Music Hall. People were definitely out to cause him trouble.

One evening, when the music hall was full, someone in the crowd mischievously called out, 'Fire. Fire.' People panicked and stampeded for the exits. Before it was realised that the call was a hoax, several people had been crushed to death. Spurgeon never recovered from the shock of the event. For years afterwards, the memory would bring him to tears.

However, the work went on and in 1857 two further things of note took place. Spurgeon founded a college for pastors. It was set up to train those who otherwise might not have been able to afford a theological education. As a result many Baptist congregations were planted throughout London and missionaries were sent all over the world. Then at the Crystal Palace in London, Charles spoke to his largest ever congregation numbering 23,654 people, not before speaking to a much smaller audience, an audience of one.

Two days before the event, Charles wanted to see what the auditorium was like. Were the acoustics good enough and would his voice carry to the back of the hall? He paid a visit to Crystal Palace where the event was due to take place and on the podium he cried out in a loud voice, 'Behold the Lamb of God, which taketh away the sin of the world.' Unknown to him in one of the galleries, a workman was there with his tools and overheard the preacher. There and then he was convicted of his sin and immediately stopped what he was doing and went home to pray.

In 1861, Spurgeon's congregation had to move again to new purpose-built premises. This venue was named the Metropolitan Tabernacle and it is still a place of worship today.

Preaching and writing were the key parts of Spurgeon's ministry, but he also founded an orphanage, widows' refuges, and a home for women suffering from domestic abuse. Charles was also a passionate abolitionist against slavery. Not even threatening letters against him would persuade Spurgeon to change his position on this issue: 'I do from my inmost soul detest slavery ... Whenever a slave-holder has called upon me, I have considered it my duty to express my detestation of his wickedness.'

Slavery wasn't the only controversy that Spurgeon engaged with. He fiercely stood up for his fellow man while also defending the Word of God. When Spurgeon argued with his fellow Baptists about how some were treating God's Word the controversy that resulted gained the name the Downgrade Controversy. This was because Spurgeon's magazine, *The Sword and the Trowel*, used those words when describing what people were trying to do with Scripture. They were downgrading it. Spurgeon accused some Baptist preachers of denying the deity of the Son of God and rejecting the power of Christ's atoning death.

Spurgeon declared, 'Whether it be the Baptist Church, or the Episcopalian, or the Presbyterian Church which errs from Christ's way, it is nothing to any one of us which it may be; it is Christ we are to care for, and Christ's truth.'

If you've read some of the other stories in this book, you will have noticed that theological controversies like this are never far away from the church. These very issues were tackled by the Early Church and by the Reformers. Spurgeon fought against old heresies. You too may have to defend the gospel in a similar way. Very often old errors just raise their heads under new names and guises.

The Downgrade Controversy caused a great division amongst the Baptists and Spurgeon lost close friends from this disagreement. He wanted the Baptist Union to sign an Evangelical statement of faith, but the Union refused. Charles Spurgeon resigned from the Baptist Union on 28th October, 1887.

Charles preached his last sermon in June 1891 and died six months later. When he died, London went into mourning. Nearly 60,000 people came to see his body laid out in state at the Metropolitan Tabernacle. Over 100,000 people lined the streets when his funeral hearse travelled to the cemetery. Flags flew at half-mast and shops and pubs were closed. He was buried at West Norwood cemetery in Lambeth, London.

By the time of his death in 1892, he had preached nearly 3,600 sermons and published 49 different publications. A large number of these were translated into other languages such as Arabic, Armenian, Bengali, Bulgarian, Castilian, Chinese, Congolese, Czech, Dutch, Estonian, French, Gaelic, German, Hindi, Russian, Serbian, Syriac, Tamil, Telugu, Urdu, and Welsh.

It was the Word of God that was his passion and his cause – and he recognised the danger which faced the church when it did not give the Word the importance it was due. 'We shall soon have to handle truth, not with kid gloves, but with gauntlets, – the gauntlets of holy courage and integrity. Go on, ye warriors of the cross, for the King is at the head of you.'

Things to do:

1. Find a map of the world and work out where the countries are that speak the languages that Spurgeon's books and sermons were translated into.
2. In a dictionary look up the definition of the word 'downgrade'. What is the opposite of this word? How should we respond to the Word of God?
3. Look up these Bible verses Isaiah 45:22; Psalm 123:2; Micah 7:7; Hebrews 12:2. What do they have in common?

15

Hudson Taylor

(1832–1905)

Hudson Taylor was a Protestant Christian missionary to China and the founder of China Inland Mission (now OMF International).

If someone from the past was able to time travel to your hometown, do you think they would be able to blend in? If a woman from the 1800s left her century to immediately arrive in yours, she might find it difficult to walk down your street without causing some comment. Think about the clothes she would be wearing. She would look very different in ankle-length skirts, petticoats and a corset. All the other women on the street would be wearing shorter skirts, even jeans. She would talk differently and wouldn't have a clue about what a phone was, far less the internet. This time traveller would have a lot to learn before she would be able to assimilate into our society.

In the past, when foreign missionaries travelled to far off lands to share the gospel, they would do one of two things. They would either bring their culture with them, or they would attempt to adapt and integrate with the people they were hoping to reach. Pretty much every missionary would learn the language of the area, but some missionaries were willing to take it further by adopting similar clothing and hairstyles.

They realised that sometimes the way they looked and behaved could be off-putting to the local population and was therefore a hindrance to forming relationships or preaching the gospel. The hero we are going to be introduced to in this story is a missionary who became famous for cultural integration – totally changing the way he looked in order to come alongside Chinese people and tell them about the Lord Jesus Christ.

On the 21st of May, in the year 1832, a Yorkshire chemist James Taylor and his wife, Amelia, were blessed with a baby boy. James and Amelia were committed Christians and it was their sincere prayer that their children would follow the same Saviour as they did – that they would come to trust in the one true God. Their little boy, Hudson, was prayed for by the couple before he was even born. And James and Amelia even prayed that their young son would one day bring the good news of Jesus to the Chinese people – as they were both passionately concerned for that country and its need for Christ.

China was not a Christian country in the way that some countries from Europe, the Commonweath and America were. Protestant missionaries had only started to travel there in the early 1800s. However, even if you are born in a 'Christian' country that does not automatically make you a Christian. Most people are not born believers and that was certainly the case with Hudson Taylor. Although his parents taught him about his need for salvation, Hudson seemed to think that becoming a Christian was something he had to sort out all by himself. Time and time again he tried to make himself a Christian but with no joy. He eventually decided that he simply could not be saved. So, the young man decided to have his fill of life and enjoy it. He would simply wait for the punishment of sin that he was sure would come his way. What a depressing way to live!

His parents' hearts were broken as they saw their young son abandon the faith. His mother prayed desperately for the Lord God to save her son. One day, when Hudson's mother was away from home, about seventy miles or so, she felt a tremendous urge to pray for Hudson and to pray specifically for his salvation. She went to her room, locked the door, and committed to staying there in prayer until she was certain her prayers had been answered. Meanwhile at Barnsley, Yorkshire, where Hudson was enjoying a break from his usual duties at the chemist, he happened to wander into the library. There on a sideboard was a small pamphlet, a Christian publication that people called a tract. Hudson looked at it. He knew what it was, but instead of ignoring it he picked it up for a read. 'There will be a story at the beginning and then a sermon at the end. I'll read it and then put it away before it begins to preach at me.'

However, that didn't happen. While Hudson was reading he came across the phrase, 'The finished work of Christ.' Hudson wondered what it was that was finished. Hudson remembered Jesus' words on the cross, 'It is finished', and then he remembered what he had been taught from his earliest days – that Christ had died for our sins, and for the sins of the whole world. Then he asked himself, 'If Christ's work has been finished and all the debt paid, then what is left for me to do?'

'And with this dawned the joyful conviction, as light was flashed into my soul by the Holy Spirit, that there was nothing in the world to be done but to fall down on one's knees and accept this Saviour and his salvation.'

At the same time, his mother felt a great peace. She knew that her prayers had been answered. Two weeks later, when she returned home, Hudson was the first to welcome her at the door. She gave him a big hug and said, 'I know my son. I know. I have been rejoicing in your salvation these past two weeks.'

With this beginning to his Christian life, Hudson would always have a strong belief in the power of prayer.

Not long after his conversion, Hudson felt a strong call from God to devote his life to God's service. The young man didn't know where he would end up serving God but knew that this would be his life's purpose from then on. Within a few months, however, Hudson was convinced that it was China that the Lord God was calling him to. Hudson began a regime of preparation for ministry service which involved physical training and discipline. He went even as far as removing his feather mattress from his bed in order to get used to the hardships that a missionary was certain to face. Knowing that China was in great need of medical missionaries, Hudson set about planning his training. He was given the position of a medical assistant in Hull and committed himself to setting aside one tenth of his income each month to give to God as an offering. This was all in preparation for life as a missionary which Hudson Taylor knew would not be an easy one. During this training, Hudson would have to provide all his educational expenses as well as his board and lodgings. Then, as time went on, Hudson realised that he could actually survive on quite a bit less than he had originally thought so, was able to give away far more of his income than just one tenth. He survived on a very basic diet and found that enjoying less in the way of physical luxuries, gave him much more spiritual joy.

Hudson wanted to build up his faith muscles. He realised that in China he would have no one to call on except God so it was important, before leaving England, to learn how to 'move man, through God, by prayer.'

One day he was given the opportunity to put this into practice. His employer asked Hudson to remind him when his salary was due, but Hudson didn't want to do that. He felt this was not showing confidence in God. So, he left these things in the Lord's hands. Hudson asked God to remind his employer about the salary so that he would be encouraged by seeing his prayers answered.

One week the employer was several days overdue with the salary. Hudson prayed, but no salary was forthcoming. By the end of the next week, Hudson had no money left except one half crown coin. His employer left for the night and Hudson realised he had another weekend without his salary. However, God had not left him to starve before and he had confidence that he would be provided for.

On Sunday he went to church as usual and then, after the services, went to the local Gospel Mission to help with the poor. There, he met a man who pleaded with him to come back to his house to pray with his seriously sick wife. The poor man told Hudson that he had asked the local priest to come to visit, but because he couldn't pay the fee the priest had refused to come. The family didn't even have the eighteen pence that was needed to provide a priest for a sick woman. Hudson thought about the coin in his pocket. *'If only I had two then I would gladly help this man.'* When they arrived at the poor man's home, Hudson saw the squalid conditions that the family were living in. Five hungry children huddled in a corner. Their mother, laid out on a wooden box for a bed, was trying to nurse a child not two days old. In pain, and exhausted, both mother and child looked weak and lifeless. *'If only I had just a sixpence more than what I have, how willing I would be to give this family some money,'* Hudson thought. Hudson was not prepared to trust God enough to give the husband, of this sick and dying woman, his last coin.

Hudson tried to comfort the sick woman and her family with warm encouraging words, but even as he said them he thought to himself, *'You hypocrite! Telling these people that there is a loving Father in heaven, yet you are not willing to trust God yourself with your half crown!'*

He then prayed, as he had been asked, but as soon as he started his conscience accused him, *'Dare you kneel down and call God Father with that money in your pocket?'* Hudson got up from his knees in great distress. The husband of the sick woman turned to him and said, 'You see what a terrible state we are in. Is there anything you can do to help us?'

With that, Hudson reached into his pocket and gave the man the coin. 'It may seem a small thing to you that I give you this coin, as I seem so much better off than you. But believe me when I give you this coin I give you my all. And believe me also when I say that there is a loving heavenly Father that you can trust.'

With that, Hudson felt such relief. He returned to his lodgings and ate the last bit of food that he had there before turning in for the night, praying that God would provide for him by tomorrow. The following day, as he was sitting at the breakfast table, his landlady came in holding a letter. Hudson couldn't make out the handwriting and the postmark on the envelope was blurred, which meant he couldn't even work out where it had come from. On opening the envelope there was no note, just a pair of gloves. What a strange package? When Hudson tried them on for size he realised that there was something tucked inside one of the fingers – a whole half sovereign. Four times the amount of money he had given to the poor family the night before. Later that day, Hudson's employer remembered about the salary!

Hudson Taylor would say later on that this experience taught him to trust in God, because if we are faithful to God in little things, we shall gain experience and strength that will be helpful to us in the more serious trials of life.

And one of the serious trials would be his life in China. It is hard for us to imagine today what a trial leaving your home was at that time in history. We are so used to international travel these days. In Hudson Taylor's time,if you left to travel to China on a ship it would take you six months to get to your destination. If you wrote a letter on your arrival to tell your family that you had arrived safely, it would then take another six months for that letter to make its way back.

Hudson Taylor joined the Chinese Evangelisation Society and on the 19th of September, 1853, he left the shores of England, waving to his weeping mother who stood on the pier at Liverpool. Neither expected to see the other again in their lifetime. Hudson arrived in Shangai, China on the 1st March, 1854. It was a different year, a different city, a different continent – and quite a different world. He had already begun his studies of the Chinese language before his arrival and had brought with him some medical supplies. However, he still had something to learn. As he tried to preach to the Chinese people he soon began to realise they didn't want anything to do with him. They described him as a dark devil. Hudson realised that his appearance was standing in the way of his sharing the gospel. That was when he decided to wear Chinese clothes and even grow his hair into a pigtail. He was blonde so he had to dye it – and in order to look like a real Chinese man he had to shave his head in a particular way at the front.

It made things easier, but not that easy. Once, all his medical supplies were destroyed in a fire and another time, as he travelled across China, he was robbed of pretty much everything he owned. In 1857 Hudson and some other missionaries realised that the mission board that they had joined was not helping them. They resigned and started a new mission.

In 1858, Hudson Taylor married Maria Dyer and they began a missionary work in China together, taking over the hospital in the town of Ningbo. However, in 1860, because of ill health, it was decided that Hudson, Maria and their young daughter Grace should return to England to recover. Hudson would inform the church in the United Kingdom about the need for more missionaries in China.

When back in England, Hudson helped in the translation of the New Testament into one of the Chinese dialects. He did some further medical studies and both he and Maria wrote a book called *China's Spiritual Need and Claims*. This book touched the hearts of many, even encouraging some to travel to China for themselves to be missionaries.

In June 1865, Hudson Taylor made the commitment to found a new society to reach the unreached provinces of China – this became known as the China Inland Mission.

There were no restrictions as to what denominations could join the society, provided the candidates were sound in faith and doctrine. All who went out as missionaries went in dependence on God for their physical supplies. The mission did not guarantee any income. The mission itself was supported entirely by the free will offerings of Christians. So, all its needs were laid on the Lord in prayer. No collections were taken at meetings or begging letters sent by its members.

And although some of these instructions might have sounded strange, by the time Hudson Taylor made the return journey to China in 1866 there were another twenty-one missionaries with him. This time the journey would only take four months and when they arrived back in Shanghai on 30th September, 1866, all the missionaries, men and women, were dressed in native clothing!

The struggles the young mission organisation faced were very real. There were disagreements between the candidates and Hudson and his wife knew the suffering of grief as several of their children died. Grace died from meningitis in 1867. Maria herself died from cholera in the year 1870.

In 1874 Hudson suffered a fall and was seriously ill as a result. At that time he put out an appeal for more missionaries. By 1887, after having recovered somewhat, he spoke in the United Kingdom and the United States about the need for missionaries in China. The CIM society numbered over 100 missionaries of varying denominations and backgrounds. In fact, the CIM at the time was one of the few missionary organisations who were willing to take on single women as candidates.

During the Boxer Rebellion, the mission lost 58 missionaries and 21 children to martyrdom. Hudson retired from the mission in 1902. His second wife died from cancer when Hudson Taylor was living in Switzerland. After that he made his last journey back to China in 1905. He died suddenly in the city of Changsha and was buried beside Maria in a small English cemetery near the Yangtze River.

We look on Hudson Taylor as a hero of the church – he maybe didn't see himself that way. What he is known to have said about himself and his mission was that he wished to be an example of what great things God can do through very small people.

Things to do:
1. Find Liverpool on a map or globe and trace a likely journey from there to Shanghai in China. On a map of China see if you can find Changsha and the Yangtze River.
2. In a dictionary look up the definition of the word 'missionary'. Do you think you need to go somewhere to be a missionary?
3. Look up these verses in the Bible: John 19:28-30; John 17:4. How did the lesson from these verses change Hudson Taylor?

16
George Müller
(1805—1898)

George Müller was a Christian evangelist and founder of several orphanages in Bristol, England

When you are trusted with a responsibility, you will have earned that trust by proving to others that you can be relied on. If you lose that trust, you may never gain it back as that's the way it works in our world. However, you might be surprised to learn that God's ways are not our ways. That is what it says in the Bible (Isaiah 55:8). If you have done something wrong, God can still turn you around. He did it with the Apostle Peter and the Apostle Paul. The life of George Müller is a twentieth century example that God can forgive you and give you a job to do, even if you've already made a mess of things.

George Müller was born in Kroppenstaedt, Germany on 27th September, 1805. His family was well off, perhaps too well off, as his father gave him and his brother a lot of money but no advice about how to use it. George wasted it in drinking and gambling. He thought nothing of stealing from his friends and even his own father in attempts to replace the money that he had lost at cards.

One day his father, suspecting that his son had stolen some money from him, called George into his study. He accused George of the theft. George simply denied it. His father decided to search his son but could not find any money on him, until he had the idea to search inside George's shoes. When his son reluctantly removed his footwear, his father came across the missing coins.

However, instead of being genuinely repentant, George just went from bad to worse. At sixteen years of age, George Müller was thrown in prison for not paying his hotel bills. He was there for five weeks until his father agreed to pay the bills for him. In 1825 George's father persuaded him to go to Halle University to study theology. Not that his dad had any wishes for his son to become spiritual. No, he wanted George to make his own money and thought that a career in the church would be a good way to do that.

However, while studying at university George just did what he normally did – drinking, gambling and swindling his unsuspecting friends. Once, when he and some lads decided to go on a holiday to Switzerland, George volunteered to do all the organising for the trip. He collected the money from his friends to pay for the travel and other expenses, making sure to charge his friends more than was needed so that he wouldn't have to pay so much.

The thing was that one of George's friends named Beta was not like George. Beta was quiet and studious and a bit dull. Beta didn't like that and came on the holiday because he wanted to be more like George and have fun. However, when he was on the holiday he realised that this 'fun' wasn't fun after all. When he and George were out on a walk towards the end of the break, Beta happened to mention that on his return he would be attending a Bible study with some other friends. 'What do you do at that?' George asked. 'We read the Bible and pray,' was the simple reply.

'Oh, that sounds interesting,' George remarked. 'I think I'll come with you.'

Beta was doubtful but was finally persuaded to take George with him to the study. Beta was a bit nervous that George would just make fun of them all. However, the truth was that George was truly concerned about his soul. He was convinced that he really needed to be on a better footing with God. Every time he took communion he promised God that he'd turn himself around, but nothing ever stuck. Perhaps this Bible study would help?

The study was quite an eye opener to George. When people prayed they went on their knees. They talked about God loving them. The leader of the study closed the meeting in prayer and George thought how he could never pray as well as that man. 'And yet I've had all this education in theology and he has none?'

For the first time, George Müller came to understand the meaning of the Bible verse John 3:16: 'For God so loved the world that he gave his only begotten Son that whosoever believeth in him should not perish but have everlasting life.'

He realised that Jesus had died on the cross to take the punishment and guilt of sin that he deserved. Understanding in some small way that Jesus loved him, George knew that he must love him in return. His father and others had begged him on many occasions to give up his disgraceful lifestyle – but none of their pleadings had had any effect on George. However, one Bible study and an encounter with the Lord Jesus Christ had completely turned George's life around. Through the love and power of Christ, George rejected his life of sin.

George was different and everyone could see it. No more visits to the pub. He stopped telling lies. He stopped stealing and would pay back his debts. However, despite all these changes for the better, George only met with ridicule from friends or anger from his family. When he eventually asked his father for permission to be a missionary, the man was livid! He hadn't sent his son to university in order for him to go off and serve God as a penniless missionary. 'If you do this then I will no longer call you my son!' Mr. Müller made his opinions quite clear on the matter.

George went back to his university studies determined to do so without the help of his father's money. This was the beginning of George's commitment to trusting in God for his needs and in the power of prayer. And George's prayers were answered. The money he needed was supplied when a lecturer asked him to help three American professors with their German. He became something like an assistant to them, was paid for it, and at the same time was able to learn the English language. Something that would stand him in good stead later on.

At the same time, George was given lodgings by a Christian orphanage in exchange for some basic work and assistance. Working at the orphanage showed George a different way of living and working for God – that all your needs can be met through prayer. This was something that George would model in his own missionary work in the future.

George finally decided to join the London Missionary Society in order to be a missionary to Jewish people, but there were a couple of hurdles to overcome. To join the mission he needed his father's permission, and he still had a year of military service to do for the Prussian state. Every man had to commit to that. Then, George also became very unwell. As it turned out, the last problem sorted out the issue of military service as he was so unwell the army didn't want him. George was free to join the mission after all and as his father had mellowed over the last couple of years, he gave George the permission he needed to go. George set sail for England which was the land God had chosen George to work in.

In the end, the missionary work that George gave his life to was different to what he had originally thought it would be. God's plans took him on a different route after meeting another missionary named Henry Craik. They both felt a calling towards children's work. And in 1832, after George had married a woman named Mary Groves, he and Henry found themselves in Bristol as pastors to two neighbouring churches. In 1835, George was led to start an orphanage much like the one he had been involved with in Germany.

There had been a terrible cholera epidemic and Bristol's streets were filled with orphaned children, homeless and hungry. George stepped in by calling a public meeting, with the aim of opening a home for orphans. George had no funds and had no idea of where he would get them either, but God had promised to provide. Four days before the meeting, George had read Psalm 81:10 and knew that God was speaking directly to him. 'Open your mouth wide and I will fill it.'

Within five months the £1,000 that was needed to start the home had been provided. Qualified staff had volunteered their services free of charge. The first home opened on 11th April, 1836. Other homes would follow for boys and girls, where they would be fed and educated and taught about the Lord Jesus Christ.

By the year 1846, George Müller had three different houses on the one street in Bristol, all accommodating orphan children. Some of his neigbours complained. George decided it was time to purchase land so that they could build their own orphanage. To accomplish this they needed the massive sum of £10,000. George did what he always did and prayed. His prayers were answered. They managed to buy a site in the country, just outside the city and the land was bought at well below the asking price. The orphanage of Ashley Down began. The architect agreed to do his work free of charge. And in 1849 the first house was completed – debt free.

That became typical of all of George Müller's work. He refused to build anything unless the funds were there, but that never stopped the work. The funds for anything – buildings, provisions, even food were always provided in time. The orphanages run by George never owed anything.

From the beginning of George's Christian life he had trusted in God to provide. Whenever George found himself, his family, or the ministry in need, he simply brought his needs before the Lord in prayer; often finding that even before he had prayed God had been working behind the scenes. Men and women would come up to George to give him just what was needed by way of money or provisions – and without George even asking. They would then say how God had prompted them to do it.

When he started the first orphanage, George began to make a list of the many and varied donations they received: ten basins, eight mugs, one plate, five desert spoons, six teaspoons, one pillow case; one tablecloth; also one pound. Donations came in from rich and poor ... a lot of the time from the poor. The members of George's own congregation were not rich people, but they gave freely of what little they had. And every donation was gratefully received and George thanked the Lord.

One donation, that George received, was from a poor seamstress who had been given an inheritance of £100 that she wished to give to the orphanage fund. George was concerned that she could not afford to give away such a large sum and would eventually regret it. The woman would not be persuaded. 'If the Lord Jesus Christ gave his last drop of blood for me, how can I not give him this £100?'

One of the first legacies the orphanage received was from a young boy himself, who, when he knew he was dying, gave the few savings that he had accumulated into the funds of the orphanage: six shillings and six and a half pence.

Through seeing God at work and in reading Psalm 68:5, George could claim God's promise for fatherless children. 'He is their Father and has therefore pledged himself to provide for them and care for them and I have only to remind him of the need of these poor children in order to have it supplied.'

Now, do you remember the teenage George who stole money and ended up in jail for five weeks? What a change came over him. During his work with the orphans in Bristol, George was entrusted with the use of hundreds of thousands of pounds. And over the years of his work, George Müller meticulously recorded every penny that was ever given to him through donations, gifts, and wages.

After his own death, the accounts of the orphanages and charities he was involved in revealed the extent of his own donations to the cause. Over the years he had anonymously given from his own funds over £80,000. Money that he had been given for his personal needs.

The stories of the frequent and amazing ways that God provided for George and the orphans fill whole chapters of books that have been published about this man's life and ministry.

There was the time that the orphanage needed to be repaired in the middle of winter. The builders were ready to do the repairs, but the heating would have to be turned off in order to complete the work. George and the staff prayed. The north wind was howling, but these orphans belonged to the Lord. Just as the work began, an unseasonable spell of warm weather unfurled – meaning that the work was done quickly and with no hardship to the children or staff.

In the middle of all the struggles and lack of funds, no child ever missed a meal, ever went barefoot or ever found themselves lacking medical assistance. They all benefited from an excellent education. The standard was so high that some local businesses complained that it was much harder now to get unskilled labourers because George Müller was educating the orphans so well!

George Müller's work for the Lord extended beyond the Bristol orphanages as he also gave away more than 250,000 Bibles. When he died he had very little left in the way of personal funds.

On his death on 10th March, 1898, when he was ninety-two years old, the British newspaper the *Daily Telegraph* wrote in his obituary that George Müller 'had robbed the cruel streets of thousands of victims'. The City of Bristol came to a standstill for his funeral.

George Müller had begun his life stealing money and would have been the last person anyone would have trusted with millions – yet God's plans are not our plans. George was used by God to steal children from the jaws of poverty and death.

God's plans are often surprising, and they are always right.

Things to do:
1. On a map of Germany find the area that was once Prussia. Isn't it amazing to think that George was an immigrant – yet by the time of his death thousands of English orphans had been rescued by him.
2. In a dictionary find the definition of the word 'orphan' and the word 'adopt' or 'adoption'.
3. In the Bible look up the following verses: Psalm 68:5; Deuteronomy 10:18; Isaiah 1:17; Zechariah 7:10.

17

C.T. Studd

(1860—1931)

Charles Thomas Studd was a British missionary and cricketer

Every nation has its national pastime or sport. In the United States it might be American football or baseball. In Canada it's ice hockey. There are several sports in the United Kingdom that could be described as national obsessions, such as football or soccer, rugby or in England it could be described as cricket: A bat and ball game played between two teams of eleven players. That is where my knowledge of the sport ends, but today's hero, C.T. Studd was a lot more knowledgeable. As a cricketer, he played for England in 1882, but this match was won by the other team: Australia. If you know a bit about cricket history you might know that this was the game which began a particular cricket competition called: the Ashes.

C.T.'s family was well off and as a result could afford to have quite a few pastimes. He and his brothers were strapped into the saddle as young lads and given little red coats to go fox-hunting. His father, who was very wealthy, made a paddock into a cricket ground so his boys could play the sport when they were home from school. Mr. Studd was so keen on horses that he bought them and trained them to race whenever he saw one that was any good. One of his horses even won the Grand National – another British sporting event that people get very enthusiastic about!

When C.T.'s father was reading the newspaper one day, he saw that D.L. Moody was coming to London to preach. He also noticed that every single news journalist had something nasty to say about Moody. This amused him greatly. There and then he decided that he was going to go and hear this preacher. 'There must be something good about the fellow otherwise the newspapers wouldn't criticise him so much!'

When a friend finally took him to hear Moody, Mr. Studd listened raptly to everything that he had to say. 'This man has just told me everything that I have ever done,' he said. Mr. Studd's life completely changed to the astonishment of his friends and family. He sold every one of his race horses and stopped all gambling. All he cared for now was that other people would come to Christ and be saved as he had been. When a family guest asked the coachman if Mr. Studd had become religious the reply was, 'Well we're not exactly sure what has happened. He has the same skin for sure but there is a new man inside.'

The first that Mr. Studd's three sons heard of what had happened, was when their father invited them to town for the theatre. They thought it would be for a musical show or perhaps a comedy, but it turned out to be a sermon by the American pastor, D.L. Moody. The boys were astonished. As C.T. said later on, they had always been brought up to go to church, but it had never been anything more than that. Church was something for Sundays and C.T. was always rather relieved when Monday came. From then on C.T. and his brothers could not escape their father's evangelistic passion. Instead of horse racing as his main purpose, it was now saving souls and everyone in his family was in his sights.

The following summer, C.T. and his brothers were home from boarding school ready for a season of fun and cricket. Their father always invited different Christian men to the family home for the weekend, so that these men would give a sermon or talk later. One of the gentlemen was not the sort of guy the Studd boys had any time for – they thought he was a bit of a wimp or what they liked to call a 'milk-sop'. Anyone who wasn't into cricket or hunting didn't amount to much in their estimation. The boys did their best to make life miserable for the poor fellow, but in the end he was the one that God used to turn each of the Studd lads to himself. He got each one on his own and shared the gospel with them, challenging them about the condition of their own soul. He asked C.T. point blank if he was a Christian, to which C.T. replied, 'Well I am not what you call a Christian, though I have believed in Jesus Christ since I was knee high and I believe in the church too.'

C.T. thought he'd be able to get away from any more talk, but the Christian gentleman was not going to give up so easily. He cornered him again, 'Do you believe that God so loved the world that he gave his only begotten son that whosoever believes in him should not perish but have everlasting life?'

C.T. nodded.

'Do you believe that Jesus died?' 'Yes.'

'Do you believe that Jesus died for you?' 'Yes.'

'Do you believe in everlasting life?' 'No,' C.T. replied. 'I don't believe that.'

The gentleman pointed out that C.T. was making God out to be liar. C.T. was being inconsistent in believing one half of the verse and not the other. C.T. thought about it and realised that he would have very little self-respect if he walked out of that room believing as he did, being as inconsistent as he was.

'Don't you see that eternal life is a gift from God?' the gentleman continued. 'If someone offers you a gift at Christmas what do you do?'

C.T. thought and said, 'Well, I take the gift and say, "Thank you."'

'Exactly, will you not say, "Thank you" to God for this gift?'

Right there and then peace came into C.T.'s soul.

He wrote a letter about it to his father on his return to school. Then one morning, when he and his two brothers were at the breakfast table, a letter addressed to all three of them arrived. They opened it to read their father's great delight that all three of his sons had come to faith. Neither boy had mentioned what had happened to anyone else – so the three lads were astonished to find out that they were all now born-again.

The milk-sop they had all looked down on as being a bit of a waste of space turned out to be the best sportsman of all, if catching souls is your sport and not fish, or foxes!

That year when all three of them were in boarding school at Eton, they joined the cricket team and their other passion was Bible study. They started one of their own which was attended by several other boys, some of whom went on to become Christians themselves. When he left the school

C.T.'s report was that he probably could have studied more but, because he was such a charming character, they were all rather sorry to see him go.

C.T.'s comment about his school days was that he learned more from cricket than he did from books! He went on to study at Cambridge University and to play cricket for England in 1882. His cricketing career was nothing short of brilliant and he was described as being one of the greatest all round players the sport had ever produced.

The sport of cricket, C.T. said in later years, taught him endurance, discipline and courage. The one thing that C.T. regretted, though, was that over time he had allowed cricket to take prime importance in his life and not Christ. C.T. had backslidden and his life had lost its primary commitment to the gospel.

'Instead of going and telling others about the gospel, I was selfish and kept the knowledge to myself. The result was that gradually my love began to grow cold and the love of the world began to come in.' C.T. spent six years in that state, but during that time two old ladies were praying for him. Then it seemed that his brother was dying. C.T. could see that now all the other things like cricket and pleasure meant nothing to his brother. All his brother cared for was God's Word and the Lord Jesus Christ. C.T. was taught a valuable lesson and was thankful when his brother recovered. 'I knew that cricket would not last, and honour would not last, and nothing in this world would last, but it was worthwhile living for the world to come.'

His life was turned back to Christ when he went to listen to D.L. Moody once again and agreed to work for Moody in sharing the gospel. This work gave him great joy and he went on to be used in bringing some of his cricketing friends to faith. One of the meetings that C.T. and his brothers spoke at was when a future missionary, Wilfred Grenfell, came to faith. He would write about that experience later: 'They were natural athletes and I felt I could listen to them.'

When D.L. Moody left to go back to America, C.T. was uncertain about what he should do with his life. He wondered about trying for a profession, but that didn't rest well with him. How could he devote his life to accumulating wealth as a lawyer, when he already had enough wealth to satisfy most? There were also so many in need of the gospel! C.T. eventually knew that he must consult God and God alone about his future life. On his own, in his room, he realised that he had been keeping back from God what belonged to God alone. 'I had been bought with the price of the precious blood of the Lord Jesus and I had kept back myself from him and had not wholly yielded. As soon as I found this out I went on my knees and gave myself to God.'

It was not long after that, that C.T. felt led to go to China as a missionary. He and six other young men who had felt the call to missionary service after listening to D.L.Moody set off for China together. They became known as the Cambridge Seven.

C.T. believed that God would provide for a Christian's needs and he was willing to live by that belief. When his father died, while he was in China, C.T. gave away his inheritance of £29,000 to be used by various Christian charities such as the Moody Bible Institute, George Müller's work with orphans and other charities in Whitechapel London and India.

While C.T. was in China he met a young woman named Priscilla and they got married. The couple, over time, welcomed four little girls into their family. C.T. was delighted, as it proved a valuable tool to teach the Chinese people about the value of women and girls – that God didn't just bless families with boys but with both genders.

C.T. began a life of missions work that would last until his death at the age of seventy. However, this life and work didn't remain within one country. C.T. felt called to other areas of the world, such as India and Africa. He was a pastor in Southern India between 1900 and 1906. In 1910 he went to the Sudan and set up the Heart of Africa Mission. Studd visited the Belgian Congo in 1913 and he established four mission stations. In 1913 C.T. founded a missionary organisation which is now called Worlwide Evangelisation for Christ or WEC International – an organisation that works across the whole world today.

The life of a missionary across multiple continents took it out on C.T.'s health, but one of the quotes that C.T. is remembered for, sums up his attitude to life and service: 'If Jesus Christ be God and died for me, then no sacrifice can be too great for me to make for him.'

C.T.'s passion for sharing the gospel meant that wherever he saw a need, he wanted to see it met. This is summed up by a little poem he wrote:

'Some wish to live within the sound
Of church or chapel bell.
I want to run a Rescue Shop
Within a yard of hell.'

'The work that God gives me to do I will strive to accomplish or die in the attempt.'

C.T. Studd died on the mission field in 1931 – the last word he wrote and said was 'Hallelujah'.

Things to do:

1. On a globe or map of the world look at the different continents that Worldwide Evangelisation for Christ works in today: Africa; Americas; Asia; Central Asia; Europe; Middle East and North Africa; Oceania.

2. In a dictionary find the definition of the word 'international'. Does that describe C.T. Studd in any way?

3. How did C.T.'s life obey Jesus' command of Mark 16:15?

MODERN DAY

18
Dietrich Bonhoeffer

(1906—1945)

Dietrich Bonhoeffer was a Lutheran pastor, theologian, writer and anti-Nazi dissident. He was also a key founding member of the Confessing Church in Germany during World War II.

Everything in our life becomes history at some point. You could argue that yesterday is now history and that today will go that way tomorrow. As we read through the lives of different Christian heroes, we eventually come to a time that is within living memory. You may not have lived during the Second World War, but it is possible that you know people in their seventies or eighties who remember what it was like to be a child during that time. If they lived in the United Kingdom, some may have vague memories of ration books. If they are older, they may have experienced air raid shelters or being evacuated from their homes. They may remember family members who fought in battles or served in other ways. If you and your family are from the United States or Canada, it may be that an older generation remember people who left their home to fight in the army, or navy in Europe or the Pacific ... the battles stretched from one end of the globe to the other crossing continents and oceans.

The Second World War was a global war that lasted from 1939 to 1945. It involved more than 100 million personnel from over thirty different nations. It was the most violent conflict in human history and resulted in over 75 million fatalities, most of which were civilian rather than military. Conflicts can happen for many reasons, but the root of this particular war was the ruling regime in Germany at that time. Germany was run by a fascist dictatorship under the direct charge of Adolf Hitler. The Nazi Political Party he was responsible for caused the genocide of tens of millions of people, most of whom were Jews. This came to be known as the Holocaust.

Dietrich Bonhoeffer became one of the central figures of the Christian Resistance against the Nazi regime in his country – and this cost him his life.

On the 4th of February, 1906, Dietrich was born in Breslau (now called Wroclaw) in Germany. He was a twin as on the same day his sister, Sabine, was also born. They had other siblings and were part of a warm and well-off family who encouraged each of the children to stand up for the rights of the poor and underprivileged. The Bonhoeffers, however, were not a churchgoing family, although the parents did teach their children Bible stories.

Questions about life and death, however, were never far away from Dietrich's thoughts. He lived in what would end up being a very violent century. For a start, in 1914 there was the First World War. Dietrich and his sister, Sabine, were young children then, only eight years old. And when the newspapers started to advertise the death figures from the frontline trenches, the two children wondered what it must be like to die. They had long conversations about eternity – especially after their elder brother was killed at the front in the spring of 1918. Dietrich was terrified at the thought of dying and that was the beginning of his search for God.

He would often have in-depth conversations about religion with his friends. Some would say later that it was always Dietrich who answered their questions, but then he would ask another question so that the conversation continued and went deeper into the issues. Dietrich hated small talk about petty issues and was serious and thoughtful as well as being fun. One day when a teacher at school asked the class what they wanted to do when they grew up, Dietrich replied that he wanted to study theology. *'Now that I've committed to that,'* he thought, *'there's no going back.'* Even when his brothers teased him about his choice he didn't give in.

'You're good at sports. Even the girls say you are good looking and you pass all your exams at school. You could do anything you want! Don't choose the church!' his brothers laughed. But Dietrich had made his mind up.

At seventeen years of age he surprised his family and went to Tuebingen University to begin religious studies. In 1924 he moved to Berlin and while there started to do some practical Christian work in a local church amongst the children there. Though he loved his studies and his work with the church, he also enjoyed socialising and would take part in sporting competitions such as high jump. Because he had to wait until he was twenty-five years old before entering the church as a fully qualified pastor, Dietrich spent some time in the United States after passing his exams and studied at Union Theological Seminary in New York.

Travelling to new countries and cultures often opens up our eyes and thoughts with new experiences. Dietrich was surprised at how informal everything was in America, but not everything was as new and exciting as he at first thought. He made a good friend in an African American student called Frank Fisher. The two got on really well and had great conversations. However, when Dietrich took his friend to eat at an expensive restaurant he was told that his friend could not be served because he was black. Dietrich was furious and walked out in protest. It was his first experience of racial segregation in America, but it wasn't his last experience of discrimination, far from it.

It wasn't long before Dietrich was drawn deeper into the black community through their passionate Christian life and worship. The people he met through this community showed deep joy in their Christian faith, despite the struggles and the poverty that they faced. Every Sunday, Dietrich went to worship in a large Baptist church in Harlem and he was soon involved in the Christian work there through a Sunday school and leading a women's Bible study class.

If there is a particular date that we can say is when Dietrich was converted, it could be sometime in 1931 – although his own writings don't really refer to it that much. Dietrich didn't really like conversion testimonies. Perhaps because he didn't really have a definite one himself. However, at some point in 1931 he did have an experience which had a profound change on his life. This happened after he had read God's Word. After this his relationship with God's Word was changed for his lifetime. He would read it and meditate on it every day. It would inspire him and what he wrote. However, there is one thing that you will find with Dietrich's writing and theology – many disagree with him. With all writings of any believer you must carefully read them alongside God's Word. Read Dietrich's words with care, but read his life with conviction that Christians need to live the Word of God.

And this is what Dietrich did on his return to his homeland. By late 1931, Dietrich had returned once again to Germany. It was a nation in economic downturn. Seven million people were unemployed and Dietrich despaired at how ineffective the church was in giving any help or guidance. When Dietrich became a fully fledged minister, he committed himself to preaching about the gospel and not just about social issues. He pointed out to people that they owed salvation to Jesus Christ, that he had died for their sins. And people flocked to hear him.

Sometimes, though, his congregations were a bit more challenging. In 1931 he was asked to take charge of a Bible study class of fifty boisterous boys. They all came from tough working class backgrounds. When Dietrich first met the group, an elderly pastor showed him the way to the classroom. He had to try and push the boys into the class as they preferred to hang off the banisters and throw rubbish at anyone making their way up the stairs. It took a while to get them in and as soon as all the boys were seated, the old pastor turned and left the new guy to survive as best he could.

Dietrich took a deep breath and decided just to quietly watch the boys until the shouting and rowdy behaviour calmed down. Speaking very quietly, so that only the boys who were very close to him at the front could hear, Dietrich began to tell a story about Harlem, New York.

The whole class wanted to hear and everyone quietened down. At the end of the story they wanted to hear more. Dietrich told them to come back next week. So, they did.

Dietrich devoted a lot of time to the young lads in the class. He realised that the more he trusted the boys to behave the more they would – and the boys appreciated the respect Dietrich showed them.

When the time came for the boys to be accepted as adults into the church (this was called confirmation) Dietrich asked them what he should preach about. It was his responsibility to take the service that day. The boys unanimously agreed that he should preach them a warning that they would never forget.

Dietrich smiled. He wouldn't do that. That was more suitable for the boys he had known who threw things down from the banisters. These boys had changed. Instead, he said to them, 'Today you are not to be given fear of life but courage. I want to give you the hope that no one can take away from you. If God be for us who can be against us.' A verse of Scripture that Dietrich would often have to repeat to himself in the troubled days ahead.

In 1933, Adolf Hitler came to power. He promised economic solutions to solve all Germany's problems. The Nazi Party won the general election and Hitler became chancellor of Germany. Things seemed to go well at first with an upturn in the economy, but these advances were made at the cost of freedom. At least Dietrich could see that. When the Parliament buildings were burned down, Hitler used this as an excuse to tighten his grip on power. Public gatherings were forbidden and freedom of speech and freedom of the press limited. Telephones were tapped and personal post opened.

It wasn't long before Hitler started to persecute the Jewish people. Jews were banned from the civil service. Property and jobs were confiscated. By this time Dietrich's twin sister, Sabine, had married someone of Jewish ancestry and Dietrich was very worried for them.

People who stood up to Hitler were suddenly disappearing or worse. Then it became clear that Hitler's plans for power didn't stop at Germany, his eyes were set on the rest of Europe too. War was sure to follow.

In the national church, Hitler demanded that all swear oaths of loyalty to him. It seemed that Hitler wanted himself made leader of the church and not Jesus Christ. There appeared to be no limits to his ego or his evil.

Dietrich opposed Hitler's plans to place the church under state control. He warned the German Church that they were drifting away from true Christianity. However, Dietrich's opposition was too radical for some of his friends. Dietrich decided that it would be better for him to leave Germany and preach for a time in another country. He ended up as a pastor to a German congregation in London.

In 1934, Hitler forbad all pastors in Germany from criticising the government in public. Some pastors gave in, but others made an open declaration of faith, 'Jesus Christ, as he is testified to us in Holy Scripture, is the one Word of God which we have to hear and which we have to trust and obey in life and death. We promise to deliver to all men, by means of preaching and sacrament the message of the free grace of God.'

The Confessing Church of Germany had begun.

Dietrich returned to join with them. He was appointed as the director of the new Confessing Church's training college at Finkenwalde. One of the benefactors of the college was an elderly Christian lady named Ruth von Kleist-Retzow. She regularly provided for the college from her own funds and provisions. She also had a granddaughter who would, for a brief time at least, become Dietrich's fiancée.

The college had twenty-five students at first who, along with Dietrich, had refused to join the national church or swear an oath to Hitler. These men were willing to sacrifice themselves for the freedom to preach God's Word. The students at this secret seminary were under constant threat of discovery. Those who studied there would later find it difficult to gain employment and many went on to be imprisoned by the Nazi regime. In 1936, the seminary had to close after it was discovered, but, Dietrich continued to secretly train men for ministry in some of the more remote areas of Germany. It was around this time that Bonhoeffer published his best-known book, *The Cost of Discipleship*,[1] a study on the Sermon on the Mount

Persecution of the Jews[2] increased dramatically. Jewish homes, businesses and synagogues were destroyed. If you were a Jew you were denied German citizenship. In 1939, when adult men were conscripted into the armed forces Dietrich found himself in a dilemma. He did not believe in war, though he would have fought for his country if it had been a just cause. However, it was clear to him that this was not a just cause but an evil one. The only option he could see for himself was to leave Germany once again.

---

1. Bonhoeffer, Dietrich, *The Cost of Discipleship,* Pocket Books, 1995.

2. In addition to Jewish persecution anyone whose political opinion did not agree with Hitler's master race philosophy, was also persecuted. Even disabled people were treated in this way and eventually the church.

In June 1939, he set sail for America. It wasn't long, though, before Dietrich was convinced he had made the wrong decision and must return to his native land. The truth of God's Word had to be preached in Germany and he could not leave the Confessing Church to face the storm of Hitler without him.

'I will have no right to help with the rebuilding of the Christian life in Germany after the war if I do not share the trials of this time with my people.'

In March 1939, Hitler marched into Czechoslovakia. Then Germany attacked Poland in September of that year. The United Kingdom gave Hitler forty-eight hours to withdraw Germany's troops from Poland and when that deadline was not met, Britain declared war on Germany. Norway, Belgium and Holland all fell in quick succession to German troops. Then France surrendered in June 1940. The British RAF withstood the invasion attempts Hitler threw at the United Kingdom, but, it would be several years before this effort finally turned the tide against Hitler.

Dietrich's duties in the Resistance meant that he was acting somewhat like a spy. He was recruited by the Nazi-government to work in their counter-espionage department, but, this work simply gave him a cover to help the Resistance Movement. We would call that being a double agent.

News of what Hitler was attempting to do with the Jews was filtering out of the concentration camps and Dietrich attempted to get several Jewish people out of Germany to neutral Switzerland. Then in 1942, Dietrich joined a secret campaign to assassinate Hitler. Dietrich knew that the church would not condone violence like this, so before he could take part he would have to resign. Someone asked him how he could agree to take part in such a violent act. Dietrich had always been a pacifist before, but now he was convinced that active resistance against the Nazis was not only necessary but moral.

'If I saw a drunken driver racing down the street, I would not consider it my duty to bury the victims of the madman. It would be more important to wrench the wheel out of his hands. We are not to simply bandage the wounds of victims beneath the wheels of injustice, we are to drive a spoke into the wheel itself.'

Bonhoeffer's military career continued to cover him as a courier for the German Resistance Movement. He was able to pass on information to the Western allies. He could visit other countries as part of his work for the Nazis but also meet with various church and political contacts who would attempt to pass on his information to the allies. One of the people who eventually received Dietrich's communiques was the British Foreign Minister, Anthony Eden. However, a lot of what Dietrich passed on to the allies was simply ignored. The Resistance was trying to arrange a treaty or truce, but, at this point the leaders of the allies were only interested in winning the war.

On the 5th of April, 1943, Bonhoeffer was arrested and imprisoned in Tegel military prison. The assassination attempt had not succeeded and Dietrich was exposed as a member of the Resistance. It was just before this happened that Dietrich had become engaged to Maria von Wedemeyer, the granddaughter of his close friend and supporter Ruth von Kleist Retzow.

Maria's status as fiancée was invaluable once Dietrich was imprisoned, as it meant she could visit and correspond with him. She was also able to smuggle in food and messages.

Throughout his time there, Dietrich continued to place his trust in the Lord, reading God's Word and praying. That was the source of his power and his peace. 'His soul really shone in that dark place.'

However, eventually all his visitors were banned and Dietrich was transferred to another prison, Flossenbürg.

He had been, by this time, about two years in prison and not long after arriving in Flossenbürg the sound of the allied guns could be heard in the distance. Hopes were raised, but, one day the prisoners were all summoned for a quick trial and all the Resistance members, including Dietrich, were sentenced to death.

On the 9th of April, 1945, Dietrich was allowed to pray one last time. Before he was marched out naked into the prison yard, his last words were: 'This is the end—for me the beginning of life.' The boy who had had so many questions about death and eternity as a child was going to experience the reality of eternity for himself. When he was hanged, he was only thirty-nine years old.

Three weeks later Adolf Hitler committed suicide in a bunker in Berlin. A month after Dietrich's death, the allied forces had won the war.

There is no gravestone for Dietrich Bonhoeffer, as no one knows what happened to his body. However, there is a memorial stone in the church in Flossenbürg with some simple words engraved on it, 'Dietrich Bonhoeffer: A witness of Jesus Christ among his brethren.'

Things to do:

1. On a map look at all the countries in Europe today. Try if you can to find a map of Europe from before the Second World War, and then one from the years immediately after it. Compare those with the map of Europe today – you will see many changes to borders and to some names.

2. In a dictionary look up the definition of the word 'witness': how does this word apply to Dietrich Bonhoeffer's life?

3. Look up these Bible verses: Psalm 66:16; Mark 13:9; Acts 1:8 – what do these verses tell us about how Christians can be witnesses?

19

C.S. Lewis

(1898–1963)

C.S. Lewis was a British writer and theologian and a professor at Oxford and Cambridge Universities.

Few, if any, of the heroes in this book are as famous as C.S. Lewis. Many people have read his Narnia books as children, even though they have little idea about Lewis' Christian faith. The Chronicles of Narnia is a set of seven fantasy novels for children, that by the turn of the millennium had sold over 100 million copies and been translated into forty-one languages. Although the books are not Christian stories, they do explore Christian themes. Throughout the series, one character in particular jumps out of the page – Aslan the Lion – a character that is supposed to remind us in some way of the Lord Jesus Christ, but, as they say, that is another story. Let's find out about C.S.

Clive Staples Lewis was born in Belfast, Ireland, on the 29th of November, 1898. His father, Albert, was a solicitor and his mother's name was Flora. When C.S. was born there was one other boy in the family, his older brother, Warren, known to the family as 'Warnie'.

It was when the family dog, Jacksie, was killed by a car that the four-year-old C.S. Lewis decided that from then on he was to be known as Jacksie. He simply refused to answer to any other name. It took a bit of time, but eventually his family persuaded him to use the name Jack instead, so a compromise was reached. To his friends and family, C.S. Lewis would be known as 'Jack' for the rest of his life.

In 1907, when C.S. was seven years old, his family moved to a new home called 'Little Lea' in east Belfast.

It was there that C.S. and his brother,Warnie, let their imaginations grow and develop. Amongst their favourite stories as children were the classic Beatrix Potter tales of ducks and rabbits and hedgehogs. All of these animals could speak, and some wore clothes like humans. C.S. and his brother started to make up their own stories about talking animals from a land called Boxen. Something, that many years later, the adult C.S. would do again when writing the Narnia books.

One of C.S.'s fondest memories of his childhood was the 'endless books' that inhabited the corridors of the family home. However, the family home was soon to accommodate some much more tragic memories. When he was nine years old, Lewis's mother died from cancer. He was then sent away to English boarding schools for his education. One in Hertfordshire, then in Malvern, Worcestershire. Unfortunately, while he was away at school, though he was learning his books, he was also forgetting his faith. It was while he was still a child that C.S. Lewis became an atheist – meaning he did not believe in God. He got bored with Christianity, which makes you wonder what sort of Christians he was encountering. And he was also angry with God, which makes you wonder what sort of Christian teaching, if any, he really received.

He loved his studies. He particularly enjoyed reading the ancient literature of Scandinavia because something in them gave him an inner longing for 'joy'. When not in his books, he loved to be in the outdoors soaking in the beauty of nature. This inspired Lewis towards a life of creating poetry. Then in 1916, Lewis was awarded a scholarship to study at University College, Oxford.

He didn't get to stay there long, though. The year was 1917 and there was a war on – the First World War. C.S. joined the Officers Training Corps and, after being trained in a Cadet Battalion, he was given a commission in the Third Battalion of the Somerset Light Infantry. C.S. held the rank of Second Lieutenant. So, within months of having entered university, the British Army sent him off to war. On his 19th birthday, C.S. arrived at the frontline in the Somme valley in France.

The war that he took part in was one of the first truly global conflicts and one of the first times that trench warfare was used to such devastating effect. During the conflict, Lewis was injured while two of his friends were killed when a shell fell just short of its target. He was sent back to the United Kingdom to recuperate but suffered a great deal from depression and homesickness for Ireland. In the year 1918 he was demobilised from the army and allowed to go back to his studies.

Later, Lewis looked at what had happened in his life: the death of his mother, the horrors of war and his deep unhappiness. He saw that these experiences had been at the roots of his depression.

Despite this, however, on his return to Oxford he received a First in Greek and Latin literature and later excelled at

Philosophy and Ancient History and then English. In 1924 he became a Philosophy Tutor at University College and then a Fellow and Tutor in English literature at Magdalen College.

C.S.'s conversion to Christianity didn't happen quickly. And it was one of his favourite writers that sparked his interest in God. He began to read a Scottish writer George MacDonald who, as well as being an author and poet, was also a Christian minister.

C.S. had some Christian friends too, one of whom was J.R.R. Tolkien. You might have heard of him. At about the same time as C.S. was writing the Narnia books, Tolkien was writing his *Lord of the Rings* trilogy. Lewis and Tolkien enjoyed discussions and debates together. They both belonged to a writer's club called The Inklings. This group of men met together for beer and conversation, and would read whatever it was they were working on, at that time, out loud to the other members.

'But for the encouragement of C.S.L.,' Tolkien said in 1965, 'I do not think that I should ever have completed or offered for publication *The Lord of the Rings*.'

And although he didn't become a Christian at first, C.S. Lewis did abandon his atheism and believed that there must be a God.

It was simply something that he could not avoid.

'You must picture me alone in that room in Magdalen College, Oxford, night after night, feeling, whenever my mind lifted even for a second from my work, the steady, unrelenting approach of Him whom I so earnestly desired not to meet. That which I greatly feared had at last come upon me. In the Trinity Term of 1929 I gave in, and admitted that God was God, and knelt and prayed:

perhaps, that night, the most dejected and reluctant convert in all England.'[1]

It would be two more years before Lewis was converted to Christianity. Tolkien and another friend had gone on a long walk with Lewis, where they found themselves deep in conversation. Not long after that walk, C.S. and his brother, Warnie, made a trip to the zoo. When they left for the zoo, C.S. was not a Christian, but by the time they arrived, he was. Lewis then joined the Anglican Church.

He had a different war the second time round. During World War II he volunteered to train cadets but was turned down, so his war effort was spent helping evacuee children from London. He and his brother had a house named the Kilns which they co-owned with an elderly woman and her daughter. Mrs. Moore had been the mother of a close friend who had been killed during the First World War. C.S. had solemnly promised his friend that, should he die, C.S. would look after this man's family. On his friend's death, that was what C.S. Lewis did for the rest of that woman's life.

During this time, C.S. began to speak on religious programmes that were broadcast by national media and from these broadcasts the idea for a book germinated. This eventually became known as *Mere Christianity*.[2]

After the war, although he had always been an Oxford man, C.S. accepted a position at Cambridge University in 1954. In 1955, he wrote the book *Surprised by Joy* as an autobiography, although, to be honest, some of the biggest events in his life were yet to happen. Moving to

---

1. Lewis, C.S., *Surprised by Joy: The Shape of My Early Life,* Collins, 2012.

2. Lewis, C.S., *Mere Christianity*, Collins, 2012.

Cambridge was not going to be the end of change for this elderly bachelor.

He had for some time been enjoying a correspondence with a woman from America named Joy Davidman Gresham. She was a writer and from a Jewish background. One thing that Lewis and Joy had in common was that she too was a convert from atheism to Christianity. When her marriage broke down, she came to live in England with her two sons. Lewis and Joy became good friends and to help Joy out of a tricky situation, he decided to enter into a civil marriage contract with her. This was purely so that she could remain in the United Kingdom.

According to Warnie, 'Joy was the only woman whom he had met ... who had a brain which matched his own in suppleness, in width of interest, and in analytical grasp, and above all in humour and a sense of fun.'[3]

Their relationship was purely on an intellectual level at first and not what you could describe as a real marriage, but this was also to change. Joy was diagnosed with terminal bone cancer. Joy and Lewis were joined in Christian marriage at her bedside at the Churchill Hospital on 21st March, 1957.

During a time of remission from her cancer, Joy and Lewis enjoyed family life at the Kilns with Warnie, staying with them until Joy's cancer returned in 1960. This time there was no remission and Joy died. Lewis was devastated but used his gift of writing in order to process his loss and cope with his bereavement. The book was entitled *A Grief Observed*[4]. Initially, he decided to write it under a false name, as he preferred to have a certain level of anonymity. The book, after all, was so personal and dealt with such

3. Haven, Cynthia, "Lost in the shadow of C.S. Lewis' fame", SF Gate, 2006.
4. Lewis, C.S., *A Grief Observed*, Faber and Faber, 2013.

a heartbreaking experience for him. The strange thing was, though, that eventually Lewis' friends would say to him, 'I've just read this really good book and I think it would help you. It's called *A Grief Observed*.' The book was eventually published under Lewis' name after his death.

In 1963, Lewis resigned from Cambridge University due to his poor health, and on the 22nd of November of that year he passed away from kidney failure. News reports of C.S. Lewis' death were almost non-existent due to the death, fifty-five minutes after Lewis' collapse, of the American president, John F. Kennedy, who was assassinated in Dallas, Texas.

When we think about Christian heroes like C.S. Lewis, the question we always ask when we come to the end of their lives is, 'What was their legacy? What have they left behind?'

Lewis left books – a lot of writing. Several books were written in his role as Christian apologist, where he argued with atheists and others who disagreed with the Christian faith. And here is where it is always good to raise a note of caution. Every single Christian that we have met in the pages of this book, and others that we haven't, need to have their work read in the light of Scripture. Lewis was a unique man and a unique Christian. Keep that in mind, even when you are reading the Narnia titles. The same thing goes for Luther, Owen and others that we read about in Christian history. Some of these men were clearly more biblical than others, or more straightforward than others, but, each had a different set of experiences. Each had a unique set of pluses and minuses. However, many of them agreed on the fundamentals.

C.S. Lewis had a God-given ability to engage in debate in person and on the printed page. His background meant that he had a gifting to challenge educated people who had nothing better to do than pick holes in the Bible. In C.S. Lewis the Christian faith had a champion – an apologist without apology.

Remember that Lewis had a unique life story prior to his conversion. He was exposed to a vast array of different literature and philosophy. He was far more educated than many other people – yet he was able to communicate with ordinary human beings. His greatest quality was perhaps his imagination which, with his skilled writer's pen, could take people to other worlds and bring them to think about God in a deeper way – perhaps surprising them into belief through a story. There are few writers, before or since C.S. Lewis, who could defend the faith and inspire excitement as he did.

His story is one that shows you can be a hero in a library, with a book and a cup of tea.

Things to do:

1. You won't find the land of Narnia on a globe. Can you think of another Christian writer who invented a fictional/allegorical story and an imaginary world? In this man's writings all the character's names teach you something. Clue: Christian; Pliable; Faithful ...

2. In a dictionary look up the words 'fantasy', 'allegory' and 'truth'. How do each of these words come into the life of C.S. Lewis?

3. Look up these Bible verses: John 8:32; 2 Timothy 2:15; 2 Timothy 2:24-26. How do each of these verses apply to the life of C.S. Lewis?

20

Francis Schaeffer

(1912–1984)

Francis Schaeffer was an American evangelical theologian, and Presbyterian pastor. He co-founded the L'Abri community in Switzerland with his wife Edith.

Everybody is different but with similarities, or similar but with differences. C.S. Lewis was a pipe-smoking Oxford Don, Francis Schaeffer certainly didn't smoke and he was more working class than academic although his mind, as they say, was as sharp as a bacon slicer.

Francis was born on 30th January, 1912, in Germantown, Pennsylvania, U.S.A. to Franz and Bessie Schaeffer. His home life was not religious or academic. His father taught him things like carpentry and other manual skills. So, although Francis was very intelligent, he chose to study mechanical drawing and electrical construction instead of more academic subjects.

Francis did go to church because of his connection to the Scouts, but the answers he was getting from the pulpit just weren't hitting the mark. Francis thought about giving up on Christianity completely, but decided that he couldn't do that until he had read the Bible for himself.

It only took him six months. By the 3rd of September, 1930, he would write in his diary, 'All truth is from the Bible.' Francis Schaeffer had become a Christian. When he went to an evangelistic meeting, things changed even more. Francis was delighted when he heard the gospel preached in such a living and powerful way. Up to this point, Francis had thought that nobody else felt the way he felt about God's Word. Now he realised there was a whole community of Christians who believed in the Word of God.

When the evangelist asked people to make their way to the front of the tent, Francis did so and in his diary later that day wrote: 'I have decided to give my whole life to Christ unconditionally.'

It was the beginning of a life of evangelism for Francis, as the next time he came to an evangelistic meeting he brought some friends.

Francis read the Bible and found the answers to all life's questions within its pages. He believed the Bible was true, without error and believed God was the Creator.

Although Francis and his parents had planned a career of engineering for him, he began to see that he needed to study theology, that this was what God really wanted for him. Francis' parents couldn't stand the idea. On the morning that Francis was due to leave for his studies, his father pleaded with him not to go. Francis went down to the cellar to pray to God and asked God to show him through the toss of a coin. 'If it's heads I'll go.' It was heads. He then said, 'If it's tails I'll go.' He tossed the coin again and it was tails. One last time he said, 'If it's head's I'll go.' He tossed the coin and it landed on heads. The answer was plain. He went back up the stairs and said to his father, 'I have to go.'

He didn't expect any help from his father for the future, but as he exited the family home the last thing he heard his father say was, 'I'll pay your fees for the first half of the year.' Another answer to prayer.

College life wasn't easy. Francis was smaller than most young men his age. He sounded different, coming from Philadelphia, and he was going into the ministry. His Christian convictions were obvious and he got a ribbing for it. However, this didn't put Francis off sharing his faith. He simply saw how lost people were without Christ. He would persistently ask the young men in his university halls to come to a Bible study. Once, one of them laughed and said, 'Alright, if you carry me there.' Francis grabbed the man around the waist and hauled him down the stairs to the study even though he was a good few inches taller and quite a bit heavier.

It was while he was at university, that Francis met Edith Seville, who would become his wife. Edith's parents had just returned from missionary work in China. Francis and Edith both found themselves at a meeting one night, where the speaker was defending the position, 'How I know that Jesus is not the Son of God, and how I know that the Bible is not the Word of God.'

Edith was furious and jumped to her feet to put across her arguments, but Francis beat her to it. Edith turned to her friend and asked, 'Who is that boy? I didn't think there was a Bible-believing Christian in this church', to which her friend replied, 'Oh, he's Fran Schaeffer and his parents are really mean to him. They don't want him to be a minister.'

When Edith got her chance to argue with the speaker after Francis, Francis turned to his friend and asked, 'Who is that girl?' He managed to secure an introduction and Francis walked her home. It was the beginning of a relationship where they swapped books, discussed the Bible and came to realise that they loved each other, loved God and the church.

On 26th July, 1935, they were married. By this time, Francis was studying at Westminster Seminary. And while Francis studied, Edith made a living with her sewing machine. The early years of their marriage were taken up with studies, making do, helping the church, youth camps and discussion. Francis talked through all his lectures with Edith, which led to some lively conversation in the marital home. Amongst other topics, they discussed the importance of standing up for doctrine and holiness, as well as showing practical godly love to others. They were both finding their way in the church and made the decision to move from the denomination they were in, to join the Orthodox Presbyterian Church. Then later they formed a new denomination: The Bible Presbyterian Church. At the same time, Francis moved from studying at Westminster to a new seminary called Faith Seminary. Then, in 1938, Francis graduated, was ordained as a minister and called to pastor a congregation in Grove City, Pennsylvania.

It was a small congregation with eighteen members. Three years later, when he left, there were 110.

By 1941 Francis and Edith had two daughters, but that wasn't the only new birth the family experienced. Francis' father had come to Christ, after suffering a stroke. One day, when Francis was visiting him, he asked his son, 'Tell me about this Jesus of yours.'

The year 1941 saw Francis move to a congregation of 500 in Chester and then, in 1948, he took over the pastorate of a church in St. Louis, Missouri. During this time, the Second World War had started and a third daughter had been born to their growing family. They started an organisation called 'Children in Christ' which ran Bible studies for children, evangelism, as well as an annual summer school and children's rally. The rally attracted around 700 children each year. Even though all their Christian work had been based in the United States, the need for foreign missions was never far from their hearts. Edith and Francis had a mirror in their home with a map of Asia drawn on it and the words, 'Go ye into all the world ...'

One area of the world that Francis was concerned about was Europe. Surprising in some ways, because that was where the Reformation had begun, but Francis recognised that the church in Europe had drifted away from the Bible. Church leaders there believed that the Bible could have mistakes in it. Francis was sent by the Independent Board for Presbyterian Foreign Missions to find out exactly what the situation was. His travels lasted many weeks and took him through France, Germany, Switzerland, Austria, Italy, Greece, Holland, and Belgium, before ending his tour in the United Kingdom. The aim was to find out how the church in Europe was fairing and if there were Bible-believing Christians there who would be willing to begin a work to bring the churches and the people of Europe back to the Bible.

Eventually, this trip was to be the start of a bigger journey for Francis, Edith and their family. Their denomination received many requests for help from European churches, and it was finally decided that Francis, with his whole family this time, should go there. In 1948 they arrived in Rotterdam, Holland, before relocating to Switzerland, eventually finding a chalet to live in with enough room for guests.

Throughout all his work there, he shared the gospel, honestly dealt with people's intellectual questions about faith and Scripture, and showed Christ's love in his life. He also fought the heretical idea that the Bible contained the Word of God and wasn't completely the Word of God itself. All of these areas impacted his life and work, the articles and books he ended up writing and the talks he gave. His love of God and God's Word even impacted the way he looked at art and culture – it was a true passion of his. Every city he visited would always include a trip to an art gallery or museum. All these things impacted Francis' mind and interests. His conversations and intellectual discussions were soaked with faith, philosophy, the Word of God and art. He had lots of topics at his fingertips to discuss with the people that were now starting to turn up to visit him and his family in Switzerland.

If you remember the mirror in their house back in Missouri that said 'Go ye into all the world,' – well, certain things were happening in their little Swiss village that meant a lot of the world would end up coming to them.

Francis had started what was referred to as 'The Protestant Temple'. He gave English services there and several girls who attended a wealthy, nearby boarding school started to attend. A weekly meeting was started by the Schaeffers, where the girls would have their questions answered. Young people from other schools started to come too. Francis would talk about such things as 'Why I believe in God'.

However, just because he answered questions, did not mean that Francis didn't have questions himself. There was a period of two months where he really struggled and started to doubt his faith. He went back to the basics, working his way through faith, and Scripture and finding out where there had been gaps in his teaching as a young Christian. It was a time of great struggle and depression for Francis but gradually he said, 'The sun came out and the song came.'

After this crisis of faith, Francis came back to a certainty in God, but other things changed too. He was stronger and more sympathetic, so he could truly relate to others who had doubts and questions, and he could answer them without being shaken in his own convictions. Everything that he had gone through had happened for a reason, to get him ready for the next task God had for him.

The Schaeffers didn't set out to form a retreat – they were just meeting a need because a lot of people were visiting their home. It all started in 1955. One of the Schaeffer's daughters brought a friend home from university because she had 'a lot of questions'. Two other girls tagged along to enjoy the long weekend and some Schaeffer hospitality. That was in the month of May. In June of that year the Schaeffer family (now four, since a little boy had been born to them in 1952) were finally given official permits to remain in Switzerland. It had been a long running problem that was thankfully resolved. Now, there was barely a month that went by without someone arriving on their doorstep. Sometimes it was more than one, often several. Sometimes they ended up staying for weeks, if not months. It morphed from something that the Schaeffers did, to something with a real name and identity – L'Abri.

The purpose of L'Abri was to show by life and work, the existence of God and to give honest answers to honest questions. The Schaeffer's wanted to show that God is personal, infinite and really there. In the same way that Hudson Taylor and George Müller relied on God alone for their provisions, Francis and Edith relied on God for all their needs. They sent prayers to God rather than pleas for money to other Christians. And they prayed that God would bring the right people to them, the people who needed to be there, and that he would keep all other people away.

They didn't even advertise that there was a 'L'Abri' in the first place.

Years later, there are now branches of L'Abri in the United Kingdom, America, Holland, Sweden, Canada, Korea, Germany, Australia and Brazil.

People came to L'Abri for answers, and they got them, but they also received love. In the Schaeffers' home, they were introduced to the God in whom they could put their trust, the one who loved them and gave himself for them.

Every visitor who came to L'Abri was told that Christianity was true and that the Bible was the Word of God. This meant that biblical Christianity could be rationally defended. Because Christianity was true, it impacted all of life, not just the religious sphere, or Sundays. So, if you had questions or interest in arts or politics, Christianity had something to say to you.

A relationship with God was for real humans, humans who were sinners in need of salvation. L'Abri wasn't out to make super unearthly saints and it wasn't just for intellectuals either, but whenever a question was asked, however large or small, Francis would take the time to answer it. Questions about the reality of creation might have been answered like this, 'How could personality come from an impersonal being, plus time, plus chance? There has to be a personal beginning to explain all we know.' Francis often took enquirers back to creation, back to the beginning, back to their origins. To show them their true identity, that they were made in the image of God.

He also made sure people realised the reality of sin and mankind's fall. Then, as well as pointing out how Christianity made sense and was consistent, he would also point out to the unbeliever where their own beliefs were lacking. They had up to that point built their life on false foundations and Francis would pick away at those foundations until that individual had nothing left to stand on. It was a difficult experience sometimes, but necessary. When the dodgy foundations had been dealt with, then the real building could begin. However, as always, Francis and Edith believed that without love all their words would mean nothing. Love had to show the way.

It was hard and difficult work sometimes as hard and difficult people with terrible problems found their way to their door. Yet the Schaeffers knew that their purpose was to show all these people the love of God, through their words and their actions.

In 1978 Francis was diagnosed with cancer. It would be five years between his diagnosis and his eventual death – five years that was filled with even more work. L'Abri's influence had spread and Francis was engaged in speaking and defending the truth across the world. A lot of the time he was writing.

His last days were spent in America, doing speaking events but also getting treatment. When it became clear that there was nothing more that could be done for his body, Edith found a home for them both and surrounded Francis with things that reminded him of Switzerland. She played some of his favourite music by Beethoven, Bach, and Schubert. On 15th May, 1984, he breathed his last, with Handel's Messiah playing in the background.

Things to do:

1. Find on a map the different places where L'Abri is working today: the United Kingdom, America, Holland, Sweden, Canada, Korea, Germany, Australia and Brazil.

2. In a dictionary find the definition of the word 'apologist'. Name two other people in this book who were Christian apologists.

3. Psalm 119:160; John 17:17; 2 Timothy 3:16 – What do these verses tell us about what we read in the Bible.

21
Billy Graham

(1918—2018)

Billy Graham was an American evangelist and prominent evangelical leader of the twentieth century.

We are now in the twenty-first century, the century that you will influence with your work, choices and conversations. Billy Graham's life began in the twentieth century and the impact that he had on the church during that century and this, is remarkable.

His influence was great as he preached to many ordinary people, but also had the ears of prominent leaders in society. Billy Graham was asked to pray at the inauguration ceremonies of almost every U.S. president since Harry Truman. However, he is estimated to have preached to 2 billion individual people during his lifetime in 185 countries.

When you think of people with this level of influence, you might assume that they came from rich and well-connected families. However, when Billy Graham was a young lad you wouldn't have found him socialising in high society – most mornings you would have found him feeding cows. Billy began his life on a dairy farm.

Four days before the First World War ended, William Franklin Graham Jr. was born on the 7th of November, 1918, in a downstairs bedroom of the family farmhouse near Charlotte, North Carolina. His arrival didn't change that much, nor did the ending of the hostilities. Work and life went on as usual at the Graham farm. Billy's mother felt the first labour twinges but still completed a full day's work picking beans in the field.

His father, William Franklin Graham Sr., was a dairy farmer and knew the meaning of hard work. Every dollar was counted in the Graham home. Then, as well as being a place of hard work and discipline, it was a home of prayer, where God's Word was respected and the love of God proclaimed.

As a child, Billy attended church with his parents in the Associate Reformed Presbyterian Church. There was, therefore, a seriousness to the young lad based on the fact that he had been brought up to know the truth of God's Word and his need of salvation. However, Billy also knew how to have fun.

Billy enjoyed baseball, though he wasn't very good at it. All that sport really did was interfere with his homework, but he did like to read books, particularly history. By the time he had finished school, he had actually read 100 titles. His other favourite thing to read was adventure books for boys. He would try to be like one of his heroes, Tarzan, by swinging off the branches of trees and yelling at the top of his lungs. All that this really did was frighten the family horses. His father, however, reckoned that it might have helped Billy to become a preacher by powering up his lungs to speak to the huge crowds that would eventually come to hear him.

As a young teen, Billy was what you would call a bit rebellious. He didn't really pay attention to his parents' faith or their wise instruction. He would drive the family car too hard and too fast. He also had a way with girls with his blond hair, blue eyes and strong physique. One of Billy's friends once said, 'If I looked like Billy Graham, I'd have a date every weekend too.' Sometimes, Billy would be dating one girl at the start of the night and then another one by the end. But he always led a pure life as he knew that that was what his parents expected of him. Despite all of his unruly ways, he pulled his weight on the farm by getting up before dawn to milk the family cows.

When Billy Graham was sixteen years old, he went to the town of Charlotte to hear an evangelist named Mordecai Ham. He wasn't that keen to go at first, but was finally persuaded. After that he never missed a meeting! Night by night the conviction that he was a sinner in need of Christ grew stronger and stronger. Mordecai Ham had a habit of pointing at you which made Billy want to duck behind the people in front. However, as the week went on, Mordecai Ham withdrew into the background and Billy became more focused on the one who was being talked about: Jesus Christ.

Meeting after meeting came and went, but Billy was still unwilling to commit to Christ. Finally, one night he was sitting near the front and heard the words, 'God commendeth his love towards us in that while we were yet sinners Christ died for us' (Romans 5:8). Billy heard the congregation sing the hymn, 'Just as I am without one plea' and could hold back no more – he repented, turned to Christ and became a Christian.

After that, Billy wanted to know what he should do with his life. One night, as he was walking through the woods, he realised that he already had the two tools that he needed to go forward …. Right there in the forest he had God's Word and he had the power of prayer. Billy felt the calling to be a preacher and began practising for that vocation by rowing a canoe out to a small island on the river. There he would try out his preaching style on the birds, alligators and tree stumps. After High School, Billy enrolled at Florida Bible Institute. There he got involved in prayer meetings and preached at a local church. In the year 1939 he was ordained as a minister of the Southern Baptist Convention.

In 1940, Billy went to Wheaton College, an evangelical college in Illinois. Not long after his graduation, in 1943, he married a fellow student – Ruth McCue Bell, whose parents were missionaries in China. Because he wanted to be a U.S. Army chaplain, Billy accepted a call to a small Baptist church in Western Springs so that he could gain the necessary experience.

During his time as Baptist minister in Western Springs, Billy was infected with the mumps and this put an end to his plans to become a military parson. However, he did become the first full-time evangelist of Youth for Christ and this was the beginning of a life of preaching on the road, in theatres, stadiums and other places. Billy's wife, Ruth, had always felt that her young husband's calling was to be an evangelist rather than a pastor and this turned out to be the case. Billy resigned from his pastorate and took his young family to live in Montreat, North Carolina.

When Billy was taking a youth meeting there, he met a young man who would work alongside him for the rest of their lives. As it turned out, the usual music director was not there that night and they didn't have someone to fill in for him. A newly married, Cliff Barrows, who happened to be a very good singer, was attending the meeting. He was happy to do the job. It was the beginning of a strong partnership. Cliff joined Billy and others such as George Beverley Shea (a famous Christian gospel singer) and a formidable evangelism team began, that would impact the United States and the world.

Many of the mission journeys that they went on, meant weeks of separation from their families. It was because of those situations that Billy, and the other men on his team, agreed to the Modesto Manifesto. Billy had too often seen the work and witness of other evangelists collapse for moral and financial reasons. The Modesto Manifesto meant that there would always be financial accountability, they would never be in a room alone with a woman except their wife; they would never criticise local churches or pastors and they would never make false or misleading claims about the number of people converted to Christianity at their events. This, and the eventual agreement that Billy and others would draw a salary like most other preachers, meant that their mission stood out. People knew that the offerings were being made for the work and not an individual's pocket.

In the year 1949 Billy Graham began a series of revival meetings in Los Angeles. He arranged to have several large circus tents set up in a parking lot. It attracted a lot of interest from the media and this generated great interest from the public. People from all sorts of backgrounds came along to hear Billy Graham speak, but in the end they came and heard about Jesus Christ and many had their lives changed and their hearts turned towards the living, loving Saviour.

The evangelistic campaigns continued in Columbia, South Carolina, New England, Boston, Ocean City and New Jersey. Their aim was 'to take the message of Christ to all we can by every effective means available to us.'

And one of those means was by prime time national radio. However, at first Billy Graham was reluctant to do it. It required a lot of funds. He was only willing to continue with the project if the Lord answered his prayer for the full amount that was required.

'Dear Lord, you know that I believe we should do this. You know that I don't have any money. Lord you know that I don't know where the money is and that I'd go out and get it if I had the time. So it's up to you, if you want this, you'll have to prove it to me by giving me $25,000 by midnight.'

Billy didn't make a huge appeal at the meeting that night but simply mentioned the idea of the radio broadcast, and if anyone wanted to speak to him about it he would be in the office at the back of the building after the meeting. The main offering had already been gathered that evening but as people exited the building they left $100 here or $5 there – all for the radio broadcast. At the end of the meeting, $23,500 had been gathered. But Billy had been specific in his prayers for $25,000. However, when he returned to his hotel that evening, three separate envelopes had been left for him there by three different people. One envelope held a pledge for $1000, the other two had $250 each.

What an answer to prayer! However, it raised another problem. What did they do with all this money – it couldn't go into Billy or Cliff's bank account. That was when the

Billy Graham Evangelistic Association was born. Ruth, Billy and two others were the founders of the Association and it was Ruth who decided on the name of the radio broadcast. *The Hour of Decision* was born and was first broadcast on 5th November, 1950.

Billy Graham was becoming increasingly well known across the States and internationally. The year 1954 saw Billy with his family, now comprising of mother, father and four kids, not only moving house but arranging for the first Billy Graham campaign in the United Kingdom. A three-month slot of meetings was planned for March to May of 1955, and the Harringay Arena was booked for the event. That venue, however, had never been filled to capacity by one speaker for one night, far less several. The British Press were scornful of this 'Yank' who had come over to 'preach' to the British. But, on the night in question, thousands filled the 12,000 capacity arena. The building was full for the first time in its existence.

Billy preached on John 3:16 – and told the congregation 'No sin has ever escaped the eyes of God, but no sinner has ever escaped his love. There is only one way back to God and that is through Jesus Christ.'

During the first week alone, the police estimated that there were 30,000 people who failed to get into the arena. Those who wanted to be part of the Billy Graham experience began to realise that if you wanted a seat, you needed to turn up early. The venue began to fill up at least an hour before the meetings began. One person, however, could not attend the venue so requested a private meeting with Billy Graham – Winston Churchill, the famous cigar-smoking wartime Prime Minister.

When Winston asked him what in his opinion had filled the Harringay Arena for all those nights, Billy simply replied, 'It's the gospel of Christ.'

When Winston confessed to Billy that he was 'a man without hope', he also asked him, 'Do you have a real hope?' Billy responded with another question, 'Do you have hope for your own salvation?'

Winston Churchill replied, 'Frankly I think about that a great deal.'

After that, Billy explained the gospel to Winston and prayed with him.

The evangelistic campaigns continued in Germany where 16,000 people signed decision cards at the events. Billy went home, but in less than a year he was sailing back across the Atlantic for another campaign, this time in Scotland. During this six-week campaign, the Billy Graham Association broke their record for the number of people who requested counselling after the event.

At the end of the campaigns this time, another individual asked for a private audience. This time it was Queen Elizabeth II. Billy Graham was asked to preach to the Royal family at Windsor Castle.

What was the legacy after this Scottish campaign? Well, it reached 2.6 million people, through meetings and national broadcasts, 52,000 made a decision for Christ. An 18,000 seat stadium was filled night after night for six weeks. Daytime meetings were held too. Thirty-seven relay centres were set up across the whole of Scotland. In the years following the Scottish campaign, the Glasgow Bible Institute recorded a marked increase in the number of people applying to study theology, as well as people applying for ministry and missionary service.

In 1956, Billy Graham did his first campaign in India. The year 1957 saw Billy Graham preaching at evangelistic meetings in New York, a city where half the population did not attend church. One person who attended those meetings was Dr. Martin Luther King. Throughout Billy Graham's campaigns, he refused to segregate whites from blacks even in those areas of the United States where segregation was still practiced.

'There is no segregation at the foot of the cross,' was his declaration.

In the end, with so many stories that we could tell about the amazing meetings and the ever increasing numbers attending, it is good to focus on the story of one life changed.

A woman came down to the front during one of the altar calls. She committed her life to Christ, but the counsellor, who had prayed with her, sensed that there was something bothering her. Tears crept down the woman's face. 'My son is a heavy drinker and I'm afraid that he will beat me up when he hears that I've become a Christian.' Before the counsellor could say anything, a voice sounded out from behind them, 'It's O.K. Mom, I've become a Christian too.'

To bring Billy Graham's story full circle, it is probably best to end with one incident from the twenty-first century. September 11th, 2001, was a day that changed the world. Nineteen Islamic extremists hijacked four commercial jets. Two of them were deliberately crashed into the World Trade Centre in New York. One crashed into the Pentagon building and another crash landed in a field in Pennsylvania, when the passengers overpowered the hijackers. Thousands of people died in those attacks.

Although Billy Graham wasn't the pastor of a congregation, he was looked on in many ways as America's pastor. He was asked to give an address at a national day of mourning.

'No matter how hard we try, words simply cannot express the horror, the shock and the revulsion we all feel over what took place in this nation on Tuesday morning. September 11th will go down in our history as a day to remember … but today we especially come together in this service to confess our need of God. We've always needed God from the very beginning of this nation, but today we need him especially … One of the things we desperately need is a spiritual renewal in this country. We need a spiritual revival in America. And God has told us in his Word, time after time, that we are to repent of our sins and turn to him and he will bless us in a new way. There is hope for the future because of God's promises. As a Christian, I have hope, not just for this life, but for heaven and the life to come. We never know when we too will be called into eternity. I doubt if even one of those people who got on those planes or walked into the World Trade Centre or the Pentagon last Tuesday morning thought it would be the last day of their lives. It didn't occur to them. And that is why each of us needs to face our own spiritual need and commit ourselves to God and his will now … We see all around us the symbols of the cross … the cross tells us that God understands our sin and suffering for he took them upon himself in the person of Jesus. And from the cross God declares, 'I love you.' … the story does not end with the Cross for Easter points us beyond the tragedy of the Cross to the empty tomb that tells us there is hope for eternal life. Christ has conquered evil and death.

… My prayer today is that we will feel the loving arms of God wrapped around us, and will know in our hearts that he will never forsake us as we trust in him.'

At Billy Graham's final evangelistic meeting in 2005, he preached the same message that he had preached throughout his life and throughout the world: 'I have one message: that Jesus Christ came, he died on a cross, he rose again, and he asked us to repent of our sins and receive him by faith as Lord and Savior, and if we do, we have forgiveness of all of our sins.'

In 2007, aged eighty-seven, Billy Graham's wife Ruth passed away, then after suffering from ill health on 21st February, 2018, Billy Graham, aged ninety-nine, passed away in his mountain home in Montreat, North Carolina.

Let's end this story with one of Billy Graham's own quotes: 'Yes Sir, take me to the cross for I can find my way home from there.'

Things to do:
1. Billy Graham campaigns have taken place in 185 different countries – look up the following nations where campaign events have taken place. Some of them might be surprising: Congo, Burundi, Puerto Rico, Japan, South and North Korea, Mexico, China.
2. In a dictionary look up the definition of the word 'campaign' and the word 'evangelist'.
3. In the Bible look up these verses in connection with evangelists and evangelism: 2 Timothy 4:1-2; 2 Timothy 4:10-12; 1 Corinthians 9:16

Bibliography

Barnes, Timothy David, *Athanasius and Constantius: Theology and Politics in the Constantinian Empire.* Harvard University Press, 2001, p. 13.

Billy Graham Evangelistic Association, U.K., *The Story of How God Called Billy Graham,*billygraham.org.uk, Article.

Cable, Mildred, *The Fulfilment of a Dream of Pastor Hsi's,* RareBooksClub.com, 2012.

Ferguson, Sinclair, *Columba Missionary to Scotland,* Article from Tabletalk Magazine, 2006, Ligonier Ministries.

Follis, Bryan A., *Francis Schaeffer: The Pastor-evangelist,* Article, Christianity Today, 2007.

Gillies, John and Horatius Bonar, *Historical Collections Relating to Remarkable Periods of the Success of the Gospel,* Vol. 1, Franklin Classics, 2018.

Gribben, Crawford, *An Introduction to John Owen: A Christian Vision for Every Stage of Life,* Crossway Books, 2020.

Hague, William, *William Wilberforce: The Life of the Great Anti-Slave Trade Campaigner,* London: HarperPress, 2008.

Müller, George, *George Müller: My Journal;* Chapel Library, chapellibrary.org, 2014.

Needham, Nick, *2000 Years of Christ's Power,* Vol. 1. Christian Focus Publications, 2016.

Nettles, Tom, *Living by Revealed Truth: The Life and Pastoral Theology of Charles Haddon Spurgeon*, Christian Focus Publications, 2013.

Owen, John, and J. Gresham Machen, *Contending for our All: Defending Truth and Treasuring Christ in the lives of Athanasius*, IVP, 2006.

Ort, Philip, *Who is Charles Haddon Spurgeon?* Article, The Spurgeon Center, Resource Library, 2018.

Packer, J. I., *Among God's Giants: The puritan vision of the Christian life*, Kingsway Publications, 1991.

Pollock, John, *The Cambridge Seven: The true story of ordinary men used in no ordinary way*, Christian Focus Publications, 2012.

Pollock, John, *Wilberforce*, New York: St. Martin's Press, 1977.

Ritchie, Bruce, *Columba: The Faith of an Island Soldier*, Christian Focus Publications, 2019.

Roberts, Mostyn, *Francis Schaeffer Bitesize Biography*, Evangelical Press, 2016. Setterfield, Ray, *William Wilberforce's Fight Against Slavery, Article, onthisday.com, 2020.*

Schaeffer, Edith, *L'abri*, Crossway, 1993. Smith, Joan Ripley, *George Müller: Bitesize Biographies*, Book 13, Evangelical Press, 2016.

Steer, Roger, *George Müller: Delighted in God*, Christian Focus Publications, 2015.

Taylor, Geraldine, *Pastor Hsi: A struggle for Chinese Christianity*, Christian Focus Publications, 2005.

Taylor, Howard Mrs., *Pastor Hsi: Confucian Scholar and Conqueror of Demons*, Kingsley Press, 2015.

Taylor, J. Hudson, *The autobiography of Hudson Taylor: Missionary to China*, GLH Publishing, 2011.

Taylor, Justin, *An interview with OS Guiness on the 25th anniversary of Francis Schaeffer's Death*, Article, The Gospel Coalition, thegospelcoalition.org, 2009.

Thomson, Andrew, *John Owen: Prince of Puritans*, Christian Focus Publications, 2004.

Trexier, Robert and Jennifer Trafton, (compiled by), *C.S. Lewis: Did You Know?* Christian History Magazine christianhistoryinstitute.org, 2005.

Wylie, J. A. and James Anderson, *The Scots Worthies: Their Lives and Testimonies*, Ulan Press, 2012.

Other books you can read in the Christian Focus Trail Blazers series:

Augustine: The Truth Seeker
978-1-78191-296-6
Dietrich Bonhoeffer: A Spoke in the Wheel
978-1-5271-0162-3
John Calvin: After Darkness Light
978-1-78191-550-9
Billy Graham: Just Get Up Out of Your Seat
978-1-84550-095-5
C.S. Lewis: The Story Teller
978-1-85792-487-9
Martin Luther: Reformation Fire
978-1-78191-521-9

Patrick of Ireland: The Boy who Forgave
978-1-78191-677-3
John Knox: The Sharpened Sword
978-1-78191-057-3
George Müller: The Children's Champion
978-1-85792-549-4
Charles Spurgeon: Prince of Preachers
978-1-78191-529-8
Samuel Rutherford: The Law, the Prince and the Scribe
978-1-5271-0309-2
Francis and Edith Schaeffer: Taking on the World
978-1-5271-0300-9
Hudson Taylor: An Adventure Begins
978-1-78191-526-4
John Welch: The Man who couldn't be Stopped
978-1-78191-604-9
William Wilberforce: The Freedom Fighter
978-1-85792-371-1

CHRISTIAN FOCUS PUBLICATIONS

Christian Focus Christian Heritage CF4K Mentor

Christian Focus Publications publishes books for adults and children under its four main imprints: Christian Focus, CF4K, Mentor and Christian Heritage. Our books reflect our conviction that God's Word is reliable and Jesus is the way to know him, and live for ever with him.

Our children's publication list includes a Sunday School curriculum that covers pre-school to early teens, and puzzle and activity books. We also publish personal and family devotional titles, biographies and inspirational stories that children will love.

If you are looking for quality Bible teaching for children then we have an excellent range of Bible stories and age-specific theological books.

From pre-school board books to teenage apologetics, we have it covered!

Find us at our web page:
www.christianfocus.com

CF4·K
Because you're never
too young to know Jesus